VICTORIAN HOUSECATS TO KNIT

Sara Elizabeth Kellner

STACKPOLE BOOKS

Essex, Connecticut
Blue Ridge Summit, Pennsylvania

STACKPOLE BOOKS

An imprint of The Globe Pequot Publishing Group, Inc.
64 South Main Street
Essex, CT 06426
www.globepequot.com

Distributed by NATIONAL BOOK NETWORK
800-462-6420

Photography by Sara Elizabeth Kellner, except as below
iStock/Getty Images Credits: AndiPanggeleng 17, 43, 103, 127; Ann_and_Pen 135; Anna Antonova 57; asmakar 73; benoitb 75; Campwillowlake 58; Cannasue 16, 97; clu 42, 50, 56; Daxi ix–xiii, 144, 145; denisk0 144; duncan1890 34, 70; getty_dumy67 49; Hein Nouwens 12, 15; ilbusca xii, xiv, 2, 4, 6, 21, 26, 30, 32, 35, 36, 40, 41, 44, 47, 52, 55, 60, 61, 62, 64–66, 72, 77, 80, 82, 96, 98, 101, 116, 124, 126, 128, 129, 131, 137, 138, 141–43; Irina Knyazeva 93; Irina Prudnikova 3; ivan-96 79, 91, 122, 134; katia125 63, 103, 139; Katsumi Murouchi 81; klim2011 99; M_SV 9, 23, 51, 57, 93, 99, 119, 135; mapo 127; Mariia Smirnova vi; mikroman6 29, 86; Nastasic 7, 38, 54, 69, 85, 94; Nata_Slavetskaya 23, 24; NSA Digital Archive iii, iv, 10, 18, 19, 83, 95, 105, 107, 117, 120, 146; Olga_Z 51; Ortaly 9; Photos.com 118; piart 3, 37, 73, 111; Pinkypills 17; powerofforever vi, 22; prmustafa 31, 63, 81, 139; Randmaart 119; traveler1116 8, 92, 102; Vectorig 43; vgorbash 37; whitemay viii; zzorik 31

British Library Cataloguing in Publication Information available

Library of Congress Cataloging-in-Publication Data available

Names: Kellner, Sara Elizabeth, author.
Title: Victorian housecats to knit / Sara Elizabeth Kellner.
Description: Essex, Connecticut : Rowman & Littlefield Publishing Group, [2024] | Summary: "In the Victorian era, each room had a purpose, and in the imagined house of the Morgans, each room also has a feline inhabitant. Meet each cat and choose your favorites to knit: 20 cat patterns. From the cuddly and adorable Nursery Kittens to Aunt Pru's Persian, each will capture your heart and get your needles flying"— Provided by publisher.
Identifiers: LCCN 2024002688 (print) | LCCN 2024002689 (ebook) | ISBN 9780811772785 (cloth) | ISBN 9780811772792 (epub)
Subjects: LCSH: Knitting—Patterns. | Soft toys.
Classification: LCC TT825 .K4439 2024 (print) | LCC TT825 (ebook) | DDC 746.43/2041—dc23/eng/20240501
LC record available at https://lccn.loc.gov/2024002688
LC ebook record available at https://lccn.loc.gov/2024002689

First Edition

To my Dad,
who would have been so happy to see the joy
that working on this book brought me,
even though he didn't like cats.

Contents

Family Tree   *vi*
Introduction   *ix*
Pattern Notes   *x*
Abbreviations   *xiii*

PATTERNS

The Parlour Cat   3
M'Lady's Marmalade   9
Cook's Cat   17
The Porch Cat   23
Miss Trudy's Tortie   31
The Garden Cat   37
The Carriage House Cat   43
Miss Morgan's Manx   51
The Window Cat   57
The Library Cat   63
Master Timmy's Tuxedo   73
The Potting Shed Cat and Kittens   81
Aunt Pru's Persian   93
Tiny Parlour Cat   99
The Gentleman's Ginger   103
The Nursery Kittens   111
Grandad's Silver Tabby   119
The Scullery Cat   127
Tiny Window Cat   135
The Fireplace Cat   139

Acknowledgments   *144*
About the Author   *145*

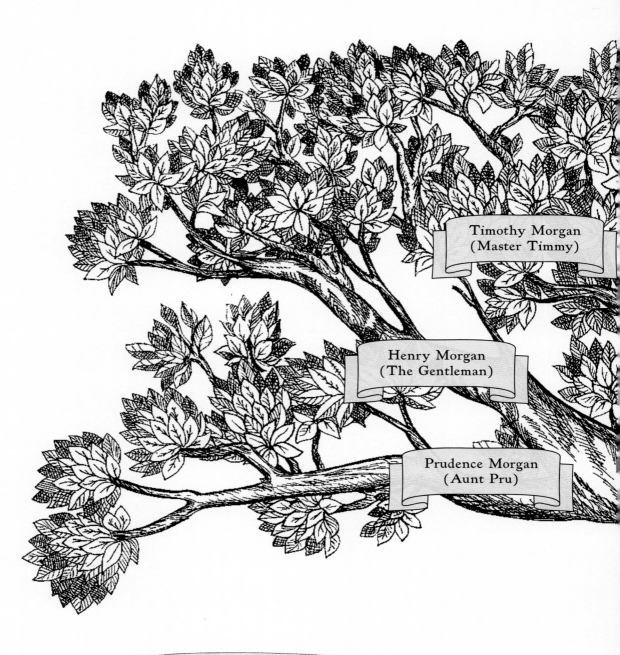

Timothy Morgan
(Master Timmy)

Henry Morgan
(The Gentleman)

Prudence Morgan
(Aunt Pru)

Morgan Family

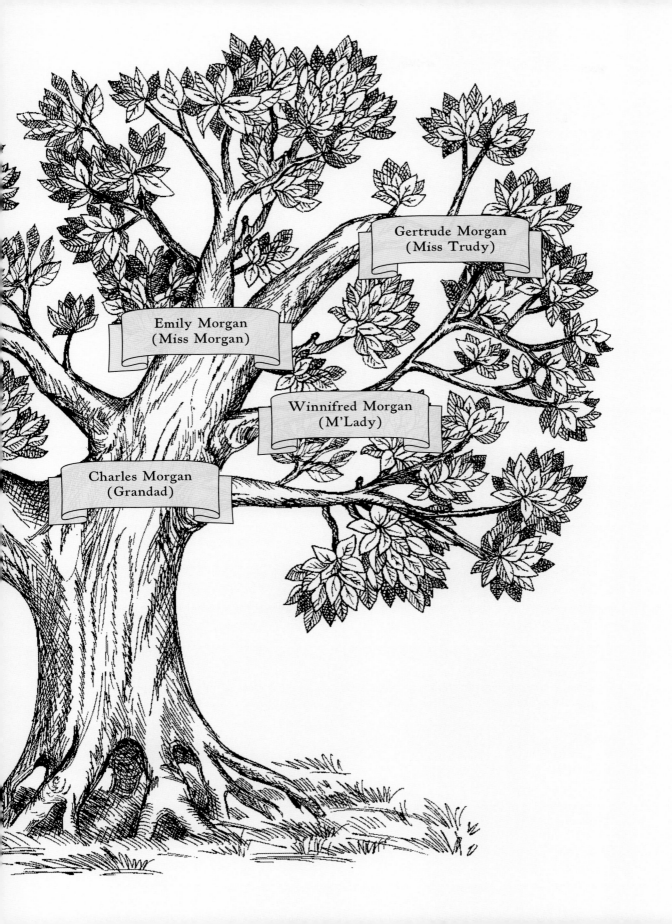

Gertrude Morgan
(Miss Trudy)

Emily Morgan
(Miss Morgan)

Winnifred Morgan
(M'Lady)

Charles Morgan
(Grandad)

Introduction

Victorian architecture is well known for several things, but one of the most interesting is the idea that each room of the large, upper-class home should be used for only one purpose. In this book, it's not the purpose but a particular inhabitant of the rooms we're most interested in.

It is believed that it was the Victorians who were responsible for changing attitudes toward domestic animals, particularly cats. Queen Victoria herself commissioned artists to paint pictures of her family cats. Cats became status symbols and an important part of the family and everyday life. It is not unimaginable, then, with all those rooms at their disposal and their desire to control what went on in them, that Victorians would have assigned a particular cat to a particular room (or family member), at least insofar as the cat would let them.

Most of the patterns in this book have sections that are worked flat and sections that are worked in the round, so your attention will always be held. A few of them are geared toward the beginner, with shaping achieved by simple increasing and decreasing. Others are more challenging, using advanced techniques, but even these aren't hard if the knitter is up for learning something new.

Cats residing in different rooms of a nineteenth-century home are fun to think about, but I couldn't write an entire book of cat knitting patterns without including a little bit about the people living alongside them, could I? So turn the pages, step inside, and have a seat in the Morgan family parlour. Don't mind the cat in there—he keeps to himself—but do watch out for the goldfish bowl. Aunt Pru will be in shortly.

Sara

Pattern Notes

I'd like to address a few things about yarn, gauge, working the patterns, and finishing details here so as not to bore anyone by repeating them on every pattern. The finishing details are all optional, of course, and knitters can make their cats look anyway they like.

Yarn: One of the yarns I chose to use for this book has been discontinued (Cascade Yarns Aereo). I learned this fact only after designing was completed. In researching substitutions, I found a very helpful website: yarnsub.com. This website suggests substitute yarns if you can't find the one called for in a pattern. It will work for any of the yarns used here and gives the knitter lots of options as well as the pros and cons of each choice.

Gauge: Gauge is not critical for a toy as it is with a garment; therefore, I've decided not to mention what my particular gauge is for any of the yarns used in this book. Gauge not being critical also means that needle size is not critical. Feel free to use the needle size of your choosing, aiming to create a fabric that is tighter than it would be for a garment. This typically means going down 2 or 3 needle sizes from what is recommended on the label of the yarn you choose. The tighter fabric will help the cat hold its position, as well as keep the stuffing from showing through the stitches of your finished project.

Haberdashery: Most of the patterns in this book call for the same small items, so I'm going to list everything you may need here rather than in each of the patterns.
- Darning needle
- Stuffing
- Scrap yarn for embroidering eyes and nose (or)
- Safety eyes and nose
- White thread, embroidery floss, or artificial whiskers
- Stitch markers

Working in the round: These patterns are written for the use of 4 or 5 double-pointed needles (dpns) and are mostly worked in the round. Different circular techniques (magic loop or two circular needles) may also work, but I haven't tried them, so I can't say for sure.

Working the pattern instructions in order: It is best to follow the instructions in the order that they are written and to wait to stuff until directed. Since many of the patterns are designed all in one piece, stuffing early can make it difficult to knit the remainder.

Leg joints: Most of the cats in this book have legs that include a joint (or "elbow"). This joint separates the upper and lower sections of the leg and redirects the work to point forward. Although the number of stitches with these joints varies from pattern to pattern, they are all worked the same way. Instructions for knitting them are

included in the patterns, but I'd like to go into a little more detail here.

After working the upper section of the leg:
1. A few short rows are worked back and forth on some of the stitches.
2. Those stitches are then divided evenly in half and placed on 2 double-pointed needles with right sides together. (The remaining stitches that were not part of the short rows are kept aside on their own needle.)
3. With the uncut working yarn, work a 3-needle bind-off on the stitches with right sides facing each other.
4. Cut yarn and pull through last stitch.
5. Turn this bit of work right side out. It will form a cup shape with the bind-off seam at the bottom/center and the unworked live stitches opposite it.
6. Stitches are now picked up along the upper edge of this cup shape to begin the lower leg. Beginning at the bind-off seam and working clockwise, pick up stitches along the upper edge of the cup shape, knit the live stitches, and then pick up stitches on the other side. You will be back at the bind-off seam, and this is the end of round (EOR) for the remainder of the leg.

Short row wraps: Picking up and knitting the wraps of short rows is a personal choice on all of these patterns; I typically do not pick them up because I believe they show less if they are left alone. There are a few instances with these designs where I think it looks better either to pick up or not, and these have been noted in the pattern. Another factor to consider in whether to pick up wraps is the yarn that is being used; yarns that are fuzzy will hide them better.

Stuffing: I use one brand of stuffing for every toy I make: Cluster Stuff by Morning Glory. I feel that this product creates a more natural look and find that it doesn't clump together as traditional polyfill does. Stuff your cat firmly unless otherwise noted, paying close attention to the photos in this book for how the cats should be shaped. A double-pointed needle is a great tool for helping to shape your cat after stuffing: Insert one end (about half, though that will vary depending on the size of your toy) into the knitted fabric from the outside. Use it to shift the stuffing into areas that need more and away from areas that are overstuffed. It's also great for bringing stuffing down into tighter places like legs and tails.

Leg supports: Some of the cats in this book are positioned so that supports are needed in the legs. These aren't recommended if the cat is to be played with, but if they are to stand on a table or shelf, you will want to use them. Any straight stick the length of the leg can be used. A few examples are popsicle sticks cut in half lengthwise, chopsticks, heavy-gauge wire, or an extra double-pointed needle. Insert into the leg from the bottom/center of the paw after your cat has been stuffed.

Eyes: I started out designing the cats for this book thinking that I would use safety eyes for all of the cats whose eyes were open. I realized after just a few designs that even though I had safety eyes with cat-shaped pupils, they still seemed to make the cats look comical. The reason for that is twofold: Safety eyes are round on top, so they bulge outward instead of lying flat against the face, and they are circular instead of almond shaped. (Kittens are somewhat of an exception to this rule because they generally have eyes that are rounder, and the tiny-sized safety eyes have very little bulging. Therefore, I think safety eyes look realistic on the Nursery Kittens.)

After realizing that I didn't want to use safety eyes on the adult cats, I was able to remove the ones that hadn't been secured with a back and embroider their eyes. The safety eyes that had been secured I had to leave in place.

One of the cats in this book (Aunt Pru's Persian) has eyes made from different colors of felt that were cut, glued together, and then glued to the cat with hot glue. My hope is that knitters will be creative and try felting, embroidering, painting, or coming up with their own unique way of making beautiful and realistic-looking cat eyes. I can't wait to see them!

Noses: By contrast, I found safety noses do look real if you get the right color. Some are bright pink; others are more subtle and natural looking.

These can be found on Etsy. They work the same as safety eyes in that they have a post for inserting from the outside and a back piece for securing from the inside. All of the safety noses shown in this book are 9 × 13 mm. That being said, I love embroidered noses, too.

Whiskers: Whiskers are optional for all of these cats; they can be made with thin white sewing thread, embroidery floss, fishing line, and so on, and they can be either left dangling or embroidered directly onto the face. I used artificial whiskers, which are available in either black or white and can be found on Etsy. The ends are simply inserted individually into each side of the nose, and the whiskers can be trimmed if desired. The only problem with these products is that they come out easily and are therefore not suitable if the cat is going to be played with.

Abbreviations

CO	cast on
dpn(s)	double-pointed needle(s)
EOR	end of round/row
K	knit
K2tog	knit 2 stitches together
Kfb	knit in the front and back of the same stitch
Kfbf	knit into the front, back, and front of same stitch
M1	make 1 stitch on the knit side (lift right leg in row below the next stitch, place on left needle, and then knit as any other stitch)
M1L	make 1 stitch leaning to the left
M1P	make 1 stitch on the purl side (lift the purl bump, place it on the left needle, and then purl as any other stitch)
M1R	make 1 stitch leaning to the right
P	purl
pm	place marker
PU	pick up and knit a new stitch from existing work
PUP	pick up and purl a new stitch from existing work
RS	right side of work
SSK	slip 2 sts knitwise one at a time, place back onto left dpn, and then knit 2 together through back loop
st(s)	stitch(es)
w&t	wrap and turn
WS	wrong side of work

Patterns

The parlour is the most ornate room in the Morgan home. It's where they keep their most cherished family heirlooms and pieces of furniture that the twins can only dream of jumping on. Mr. and Mrs. Morgan try their best to keep everyone out of the parlour except for Sundays or on special occasions; only Emily is allowed in during the week to practice the piano.

There is one cat in the Morgan family who slinks into the parlour regardless of what day it is. They let him stay because his prim and proper body language says he won't do anything he shouldn't. With paws tucked in and tail to one side, this cat tries to minimize his appearance as much as possible so as not to be noticed.

The Parlour Cat

FINISHED SIZE
- 12 in./30.5 cm long (not including tail)
- 6 in./15.25 cm wide

YARN
Cascade Aereo: 220 yd./201.25 m total (color A: 200 yd./183 m; color B: 20 yd./18.25 m)
- Light gray/white cat: 03 Silver (A); 04 Ecru (B)
- Black/white cat: 01 Jet (A); 04 Ecru (B)
- Siamese Cat: 04 Ecru (A); 07 Mocha Heather and 06 Walnut Heather (color B, per your discretion) (see photos for color placement)

NEEDLES
- US size 5/3.75 mm double-pointed needles
- US size 5/3.75 mm circular needle (optional)

INSTRUCTIONS

Body

Work begins at vertical line between chest and body. With color A, CO 52 sts onto 3 or 4 dpns (or circular needle); join sts in the round.

Rnds 1–2: K all sts.
Rnd 3: K1, M1, K2, M1, K46, M1, K2, M1, K1. (56 sts)
Rnds 4–7: K all sts.
Rnd 8: K1, M1, K2, M1, K50, M1, K2, M1, K1. (60 sts)
Rnds 9–12: K all sts.
Rnd 13: K1, M1, K2, M1, K54, M1, K2, M1, K1. (64 sts)
Rnds 14–17: K all sts.
Rnd 18: K1, M1, (K2, M1) 2 times, K54, (M1, K2) 2 times, M1, K1. (70 sts)
Rnds 19–22: K all sts.

Rnd 23: K1, M1, (K2, M1) 2 times, K60, (M1, K2) 2 times, M1, K1. (76 sts)
Rnds 24–27: K all sts.
Rnd 28: K1, M1, (K2, M1) 2 times, K66, (M1, K2) 2 times, M1, K1. (82 sts)
Rnds 29–50: K all sts.

Measure off 35 armlengths of yarn, cut, and then roll into a ball and place inside your cat's body. Place all 82 live sts onto a piece of scrap yarn.

Chest

Color B is optional for the chest. Sts are now picked up in the original CO sts to shape the chest.

Setup: Count 26 sts to the left of the first CO st. Beginning with the 27th st, PU the next 15 sts, turn work, P15. With a second dpn, continue to work on the inside of your work, PUP 15 sts in the original CO sts, turn work, K15. Working yarn is now between the 2 dpns in the bottom/center of your cat (EOR).

Short rows shape the curve of the chest.

Row 1: K4, w&t.
Row 2: P8, w&t.
Row 3: K9, w&t.
Row 4: P10, w&t.
Row 5: K11, w&t.
Row 6: P12, w&t.
Row 7: K13, w&t.
Row 8: P14, w&t.
Row 9: K15, w&t.
Row 10: P16, w&t.
Row 11: K17, w&t.
Row 12: P18, w&t.
Row 13: K19, w&t.
Row 14: P20, w&t.
Row 15: K21, w&t.
Row 16: P22, w&t.
Row 17: K23, w&t.
Row 18: P24, w&t.
Row 19: K25, w&t.
Row 20: P26, w&t.
Row 21: K27, w&t.
Row 22: P28, w&t.
Row 23: K14 (EOR).

Cut yarn.

Neck and Head

Setup: With color A, begin at 1st CO st, PU 11 sts in the original CO sts, K30 (the live chest sts), PU11 sts in the original CO sts (EOR). Join sts in the round. (52 sts)

Rnds 1–2: K all sts.
Rnd 3: K9, SSK, K2tog, K26, SSK, K2tog, K9. (48 sts)
Rnds 4–5: K all sts.

Short rows now shape the back of the neck and change the direction of the sts.

Row 1: K6, w&t.
Row 2: P12, w&t.
Row 3: K14, w&t.
Row 4: P16, w&t.
Row 5: K18, w&t.
Row 6: P20, w&t.
Row 7: K22, w&t.
Row 8: P24, w&t.
Row 9: K26, w&t.
Row 10: P28, w&t.
Row 11: K30, w&t.
Row 12: P32, w&t.

Row 13: K34, w&t.
Row 14: P36, w&t.
Row 15: K34, w&t.
Row 16: P32, w&t.
Row 17: K30, w&t.
Row 18: P28, w&t.
Row 19: K26, w&t.
Row 20: P24, w&t.
Row 21: K22, w&t.
Row 22: P20, w&t.
Row 23: K18, w&t.
Row 24: P16, w&t.
Row 25: K14, w&t.
Row 26: P12, w&t.
Row 27: K6 (EOR).

Knitting in the round is now resumed.

Rnd 1: K4, SSK, K2tog, K12, SSK, K4, K2tog, K12, SSK, K2tog, K4. (42 sts)
Rnd 2: K all sts.
Rnd 3: K3, SSK, K2tog, K10, SSK, K4, K2tog, K10, SSK, K2tog, K3. (36 sts)
Rnd 4: K all sts.
Rnd 5: K2, SSK, K2tog, K24, SSK, K2tog, K2. (32 sts)
Rnd 6: K all sts.
Rnd 7: K1, SSK, K2tog, K22, SSK, K2tog, K1. (28 sts)
Rnd 8: K all sts.
Rnd 9: SSK, K2tog, K18, w&t, P16, w&t, K18, SSK, K2tog. (24 sts)
Rnd 10: K all sts.
Rnd 11: (SSK) 6 times, (K2tog) 6 times. (12 sts)
Rnd 12: K all sts.
Rnd 13: (SSK) 3 times, (K2tog) 3 times. (6 sts)

Cut yarn, thread through remaining live sts, and pull closed.

Stuff the head and front half of body.

Rear

Place the live sts on scrap yarn back onto 3 or 4 dpns (or circular needle); join in the round.

Rnd 1: (K7, K2tog) 4 times, K10, (K7, K2tog) 4 times. (74 sts)
Rnd 2: K all sts.
Rnd 3: (K6, K2tog) 4 times, K10, (K6, K2tog) 4 times. (66 sts)
Rnd 4: K all sts.
Rnd 5: (K5, K2tog) 4 times, K10, (K5, K2tog) 4 times. (58 sts)
Rnd 6: K all sts.
Rnd 7: (K4, K2tog) 4 times, K10, (K4, K2tog) 4 times. (50 sts)
Rnd 8: K all sts.
Rnd 9: (K3, K2tog) 4 times, K10, (K3, K2tog) 4 times. (42 sts)
Rnd 10: K all sts.
Rnd 11: (K2, K2tog) 4 times, K10, (K2, K2tog) 4 times. (34 sts)
Rnd 12: K all sts.
Rnd 13: (K1, K2tog) 4 times, K10, (K1, K2tog) 4 times. (26 sts)
Rnd 14: K all sts.
Rnd 15: (K2tog) 4 times, K10, (K2tog) 4 times. (18 sts)

Do not add stuffing at this point.

Tail

Rnds 1–10: K all sts. (18 sts)

The remainder of the body is now stuffed. Stuff fully, using a dpn from the outside to shift the stuffing forward toward the head as you go. Keep the bottom of the body as flat as possible. Tail can be stuffed when completed, or a little at a time as you go.

Rnd 11: K7, SSK, K2tog, K7. (16 sts)
Rnds 12–16: K all sts.
Rnd 17: K6, SSK, K2tog, K6. (14 sts) Place a removable stitch marker on the last st worked.

K all sts in Rnds 18–66, or about 6½ in./16.5 cm from the stitch marker.

Rnd 67: K5, SSK, K2tog, K5. (12 sts)
Rnds 68–69: K all sts.
Rnd 70: K4, SSK, K2tog, K4. (10 sts)
Rnds 71–72: K all sts.
Rnd 73: K3, SSK, K2tog, K3. (8 sts)
Rnd 74: K all sts.

Stuff tail, using a dpn from the outside to shift stuffing evenly throughout. Cut yarn, thread through remaining live sts, pull closed.

Wrap tail against bottom of body along one side. Seam to body along the bottom edge from the back to about 1 in./2.5 cm from the front.

Ears (make 2 the same)

The ears are worked separately and seamed to head. Work begins at bottom of ear. CO 15 sts onto 3 dpns; join in the round.

Rnds 1–2: K all sts.
Rnd 3: K1, SSK, K2tog, K5, SSK, K2tog, K1. (11 sts)
Rnds 4–5: K all sts.
Rnd 6: SSK, K2tog, K3, SSK, K2tog. (7 sts)
Rnds 7–8: K all sts.
Rnd 9: K2tog, K3, SSK. (5 sts)

Cut yarn, thread through remaining live sts, pull closed. Flatten ear with first CO st in the center/front; decreases on the sides. Create a slight hollowing in the front and seam to head with hollowing pointed forward/outward.

Front Legs and Paws (make 2)

CO 12 sts onto 3 dpns; join in the round. K all sts for 30 rnds or about 4 in./10.25 cm. Cut yarn, thread through live sts, and pull closed.

Stuff loosely so that the paws can bend, leaving the last 1 in./2.5 cm at the open end unstuffed. Curl front of paw around and seam in place. Seam legs with curled paws touching each other to the bottom of the body.

Mrs. Winnifred Morgan often thinks that she must be the happiest person in the world. Sometimes when all her family are together, she closes her eyes just to listen to the sound of them. Laughing, talking, or even quarrelling, they're always loud, but it doesn't matter. She knows that what she has is gold and thinks that no one else could possibly be as happy as she.

Winnifred met her husband on a blind date that her friend arranged, and although he came across as stuffy at first, she agreed to go out with him a second time. It was on that second date that she saw another side of the businessman, a soft and humble side. Once during their courtship, she mentioned casually to him that her favourite scent was honeysuckle, and to this day he brings her twigs of it from the bush near the garden gate, which she presses between the pages of her favourite book. She enjoys knitting on tiny double-pointed needles and makes her husband striped socks in the colours of his alma mater.

Mrs. Morgan loves the orange marmalade that Cook puts up each winter when the oranges are in season, and she loves her marmalade cat. The same cat who, wherever she goes in their large, loud house, will follow her.

M'Lady's Marmalade

FINISHED SIZE
- 12 in./30.5 cm tall
- 5 in./12.7 cm wide
- 10 in./25.5 cm deep (not including tail)

YARN
Berroco Vintage Chunky: 220 yd./201.25 m total
(color A: 160 yd./146.25 m; color B: 60 yd./55 m)
- Cat 1: 6121 Sunny (A); 61192 Marmalade (B)
- Cat 2: 6122 Banana (A); 6121 Sunny (B)
- Cat 3: 6104 Mushroom (A); 61192 Marmalade (B)

NEEDLES
- US size 5/3.75 mm straight needles
- US size 5/3.75 mm double-pointed needles

NOTES
- The marmalade (darker color) patches and stripes
  on the chest, legs, tail, and head are suggestions
  only. Feel free to personalize your cat in these
  sections by making up your own pattern of patches
  and stripes. Those on the body, however, are
  placed purposefully in order to shape the curve
  of the back and should be worked as written.
- The front legs will require support to help
  your cat stand. A dpn or other straight
  stick should be inserted up through the
  bottom of the paw and into chest.

INSTRUCTIONS

Chest & Upper Legs

Begin by preparing a second, small ball of color A to
use in the center and 2 small (or 1 large and 1 small)
balls of color B to use on each side. All 4 strands
are carried loosely on the back side of the work.
Work begins at neckline. With color A, CO 40 sts
onto 1 straight needle. This section is worked flat in
stockinette stitch and with the intarsia method of
colorwork.

Note: Begin with the larger ball of color A.

Row 1: Color A: P40.

Row 2: Color A: K40.

Row 3 and all odd rows through Row 33: Purl all
  sts with the same color(s) as the row before. The
  total stitch count remains 40.

Row 4: Color B: K12; color A: K16; color B: K12.

Row 6: Color B: K14; color A: K12; color B: K14.

Row 8: Color B: K16; color A: K8; color B: K16.

Row 10: Color A: K40.

Row 12: Color A: K40.

Row 14: Color B: K18; color A: K4; color B: K18.
Row 16: Color A: K40.
Row 18: Color A: K40.
Row 20: Color A: K40.
Row 22: Color A: K40.
Row 24: Color B: K17; color A: K6; color B: K17.
Row 26: Color B: K15; color A: K10; color B: K15.
Row 28: Color B: K13; color A: K14; color B: K13.

Cut both strands of color B and small ball of color A now.

Row 30: Color A: K40.
Row 32: Color A: K40.
Row 33: Color A: P40.

Before proceeding to the legs, weave in loose ends on back, tightening loose stitches if needed.

Right Leg

Switch to dpns for the rest of the project.

Setup: K20; arrange on 3 dpns. Place remaining 20 sts on scrap yarn. K2 (new EOR).

Rnds 1–2: K all sts.
Rnd 3: K2tog, K16, SSK. (18 sts)
Rnds 4–5: K all sts.

Work joint.

> **Joint (both worked the same)**
>
> 1. K5, turn work.
> 2. Slip 1, P9, turn work.
> 3. Slip 1, K9, turn work.
> 4. Slip 1, P9.
> 5. Arrange sts on 2 dpns, hold side by side with right sides together.
> 6. Work a 3-needle bind-off.
> 7. Turn work right side out.

Stitches are now picked up along the top edge of work and joined with the live sts to work the bottom part of the leg.

Begin picking up sts at seam of 3-needle bind-off:

1st dpn: PU 5 sts along top left edge of work.
2nd dpn: K8 live sts.
3rd dpn: PU 5 sts along top right edge of work (EOR). (18 sts)

Join sts in the round to work the bottom of the leg.

Rnd 1: K all sts.
Rnd 2: K2tog, K14, SSK. (16 sts)
Rnds 3–4: Change to color B: K all sts.
Rnd 5: Change to color A: K all sts.
Rnd 6: K2tog, K12, SSK. (14 sts)
Rnds 7–9: K all sts.
Rnd 10: K2tog, K10, SSK. (12 sts)
Rnds 11–13: Change to color B: K all sts.
Rnd 14: K2tog, K8, SSK; cut color B. (10 sts)
Rnds 15–19: Continue with color A: K all sts.
Rnd 20: K3, (M1, K1) 5 times, K2. (15 sts)
Rnds 21–22: K all sts.
Rnd 23: K11, w&t, P7, w&t, K8, w&t, P9, w&t, K12.

Cut yarn, thread through live sts, and pull closed. Use loose end to seam hole at bottom of paw closed.

Left Leg

Setup: Place 20 sts from scrap yarn onto 3 dpns; rejoin color A, K20. Join sts in the round, K18 (new EOR).

Rnds 1–2: K all sts.
Rnd 3: K2tog, K16, SSK. (18 sts)
Rnds 4–5: K all sts.

Work joint, following instructions on page 11.

Begin picking up sts at seam of 3-needle bind-off:

1st dpn: PU 5 sts along top left edge of work.
2nd dpn: K8 live sts.
3rd dpn: PU 5 sts along top right edge of work (EOR). (18 sts)

Join sts in the round to work the bottom of the leg.

Rnd 1: Change to color B: K all sts.
Rnd 2: K2tog, K14, SSK. (16 sts)
Rnds 3–4: K all sts.
Rnd 5: Change to color A: K all sts.
Rnd 6: K2tog, K12, SSK. (14 sts)
Rnds 7–9: K all sts.
Rnd 10: K2tog, K10, SSK. (12 sts)
Rnds 11–13: Change to color B: K all sts; cut color B.
Rnd 14: Change to color A: K2tog, K8, SSK. (10 sts)
Rnds 15–19: K all sts.
Rnd 20: K3, (M1, K1) 5 times, K2. (15 sts)
Rnds 21–22: K all sts.
Rnd 23: K11, w&t, P7, w&t, K8, w&t, P9, w&t, K12.

Cut yarn, thread through live sts, and pull closed. Use loose end to seam hole at bottom of paw closed.

Body

Setup: Hold first and last CO sts together and seam top 3 rows together, forming a circle that will serve as the neck opening. Beginning at the top/center of that circle (just below the seam), and with RS facing, rejoin color A and PU the following sts along the edges of your work with 3 dpns. Additional dpns or a circular needle can be used, and sts can be rearranged on the needles after a few rounds.

1st dpn: PU 28 sts along the right edge from top/center down to the bottom of chest (PU 4 sts for every 5 rows).
2nd dpn: PU 8 sts along the edge from the last st across the bottom to the other side of the chest.
3rd dpn: PU 28 sts along the left edge from bottom up to the top/center (4 sts for every 5 rows again). (64 sts)

Note: The back is shaped with short rows, which are all worked with color B and create the marmalade patches and stripes. Picking up the wraps is recommended and is done on the first round following the short row.

Rnd 1: Color A: K all sts.
Rnd 2: Color A: K2tog, K60, SSK. (62 sts)
Rnds 3–4: Color A: K all sts.
Row 5: Color B: K2tog, K12, w&t, P13, P2tog, P12, w&t, K13. (60 sts)
Rnd 6: Color A: K all sts.
Rnd 7: Color A: K2tog, K56, SSK. (58 sts)
Rnds 8–9: Color A: K all sts.
Row 10: Color B: K2tog, K5, w&t, P6, P2tog, P5, w&t, K6. (56 sts)
Row 11: Color B: K5, w&t, P10, w&t, K5.
Row 12: Color B: K4, w&t, P8, w&t, K4.
Rnd 13: Color A: K2tog, K52, SSK. (54 sts)

Rnds 14–15: Color A: K all sts.
Row 16: Color B: K12, w&t, P24, w&t, K12.
Rnds 17–19: Color A: K all sts.
Rnd 20: Color A: K1, M1, K52, M1, K1. (56 sts)
Row 21: Color B: K10, w&t, P20, w&t, K10.
Row 22: Color B: K9, w&t, P18, w&t, K9.
Rnd 23: Color A: K1, M1, K54, M1, K1. (58 sts)
Rnd 24: Color A: K all sts.
Row 25: Color B: K8, w&t, P16, w&t, K8.
Row 26: Color B: K7, w&t, P14, w&t, K7.
Row 27: Color B: K6, w&t, P12, w&t, K6.
Rnd 28: Color A: K1, M1, K56, M1, K1. (60 sts)
Rnd 29: Color A: K all sts.
Row 30: Color B: K12, w&t, P24, w&t, K12.
Rnd 31: Color A: K1, M1, K58, M1, K1. (62 sts)
Rnd 32: Color A: K all sts.
Row 33: Color B: K6, w&t, P12, w&t, K6.
Row 34: Color B: K5, w&t, P10, w&t, K5.
Rnd 35: Color A: K1, M1, K60, M1, K1. (64 sts)
Rnd 36: Color A: K all sts.
Row 37: Color B: K10, w&t, P20, w&t, K10.
Row 38: Color B: K9, w&t, P18, w&t, K9.
Row 39: Color B: K8, w&t, P16, w&t, K8.
Rnds 40–41: Color A: K all sts.

Row 42: Color B: K8, w&t, P16, w&t, K8.
Row 43: Color B: K7, w&t, P14, w&t, K7.
Rnds 44–45: Color A: K all sts.
Row 46: Color B: K12, w&t, P24, w&t, K12.
Rnds 47–48: Color A: K all sts.
Row 49: Color B: K10, w&t, P20, w&t, K10.
Row 50: Color B: K9, w&t, P18, w&t, K9.
Row 51: Color B: K8, w&t, P16, w&t, K8; cut color B.
Rnd 52: Continue with Color A: K all sts.
Rnd 53: K60, slip last 4 sts of rnd plus first 4 sts of next rnd onto a piece of scrap yarn; CO 4 new sts to EOR. (60 sts)
Rnd 54: CO 4 new sts to working needle, K60. (64 sts)
Rnd 55: K all sts.
Rnd 56: (K6, K2tog) 8 times. (56 sts)
Rnd 57: K all sts.

Measure off about 10 armlengths of yarn; cut; roll into a ball and stick inside your cat. This will be used for working the base after the head. Place live sts on a piece of scrap yarn.

Tail

Setup: Place 8 sts from scrap yarn onto 1 dpn. Sts are now picked up around the edge of the hole and joined with the live sts to work the tail. Begin at the bottom/center of the hole and PU or knit the following with color B and 3 dpns:

1st dpn: PU 5 sts from the bottom/center of hole to the live sts.
2nd dpn: K8 live sts.
3rd dpn: PU 5 sts from live sts down to bottom/ center of hole (EOR). (18 sts)

Rnds 1–5: Color B: K all sts.
Rnd 6: Color B: K2tog, K14, SSK. (16 sts)
Rnds 7–8: Color A: K all sts.
Rnds 9–12: Color B: K all sts.
Rnd 13: Color A: K all sts.
Rnd 14: Color B: K all sts.
Rnds 15–17: Color A: K all sts.
Rnd 18: Color A: K2tog, K12, SSK. (14 sts)
Rnds 19–21: Color B: K all sts.
Rnds 22–25: Color A: K all sts.
Rnd 26: Color A: K2tog, K10, SSK. (12 sts)
Rnds 27–34: Color B: K all sts.
Rnds 35–36: Color A: K all sts.

Rnds 37–38: Color B: K all sts.
Rnds 39–43: Color A: K all sts.
Rnd 44: Color B: K all sts.
Rnds 45–47: Color A: K all sts; cut color A.
Rnds 48–53: Continuing in Color B: K all sts.
Rnd 54: K2tog, K8, SSK. (10 sts)
Rnds 55–58: K all sts.

Cut yarn, thread through remaining live sts, and pull closed.

Head

Sts are now picked up in the original CO sts to begin the head.

Setup: Begin at the center/back of neck. With color A, PU 5 sts in the first 5 CO sts, followed by 1 extra st in the back of the next st. Repeat 7 more times. (48 sts)

Row 1: Color A: K6, w&t, P12, w&t, K6.
Row 2: Color A: K8, w&t, P16, w&t, K8.
Row 3: Color B: K10, w&t, P20, w&t, K10.
Row 4: Color A: K12, w&t, P24, w&t, K12.
Row 5: Color A: K14, w&t, P28, w&t, K14.
Row 6: Color B: K16, w&t, P32, w&t, K16.
Row 7: Color B: K18, w&t, P36, w&t, K18.
Row 8: Color A: K16, w&t, P32, w&t, K16.
Row 9: Color B: K14, w&t, P28, w&t, K14; cut color B.
Row 10: Continuing with color A: K12, w&t, P24, w&t, K12.
Row 11: K10, w&t, P20, w&t, K10.
Rnd 12: K4, SSK, K2tog, K12, SSK, K4, K2tog, K12, SSK, K2tog, K4. (42 sts)
Rnd 13: K all sts.
Rnd 14: K3, SSK, K2tog, K10, SSK, K4, K2tog, K10, SSK, K2tog, K3. (36 sts)
Rnd 15: K all sts.
Rnd 16: K2, SSK, K2tog, K24, SSK, K2tog, K2. (32 sts)
Rnd 17: K all sts.
Rnd 18: K1, SSK, K2tog, K22, SSK, K2tog, K1. (28 sts)
Rnd 19: K all st.
Rnd 20: SSK, K2tog, K20, SSK, K2tog. (24 sts)

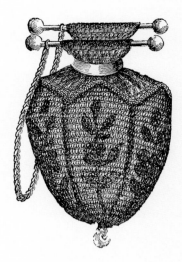

Rnd 21: K all sts.
Rnd 22: (SSK) 6 times, (K2tog) 6 times. (12 sts)
Rnd 23: K all sts.
Rnd 24: (SSK) 3 times, (K2tog) 3 times. (6 sts)

Cut, thread through remaining live sts, and pull closed. Stuff head, legs, tail, and about half of the body now.

Base

Place 56 live sts from scrap yarn back onto dpns or circular needle.

Rnd 1: Continuing with color A: (K5, K2tog) 8 times. (48 sts)
Rnd 2: K all sts.
Rnd 3: (K4, K2tog) 8 times. (40 sts)
Rnd 4: K all sts.
Rnd 5: (K3, K2tog) 8 times. (32 sts)
Rnd 6: K all sts.
Rnd 7: (K2, K2tog) 8 times. (24 sts)
Rnd 8: K all sts.
Rnd 9: (K1, K2tog) 8 times. (16 sts)
Rnd 10: K all sts.

Complete stuffing now. The body should be stuffed firmly in order to smooth out buckling of the back due to the short rows.

Cut yarn, thread through remaining live sts, and pull closed.

Ears (make 2 the same)

The ears are worked separately and seamed to head. Work begins at bottom of ear. With color A, CO 15 sts onto 3 dpns; join in the round.

Rnds 1–2: K all sts.
Rnd 3: K1, SSK, K2tog, K5, SSK, K2tog, K1.
  (11 sts)
Rnds 4–5: K all sts.
Rnd 6: SSK, K2tog, K3, SSK, K2tog. (7 sts)
Rnds 7–8: K all sts.

Cut yarn, thread through remaining live sts, pull closed. Flatten ears with the CO tail coming from one bottom corner. Bend slightly to create a slight hollowing in the front and seam to head at the first decrease on each side.

Back Legs (make 2 the same)

With color A, CO 10 sts onto 3 dpns.

Rnds 1–20: K all sts.
Rnd 21: K3, M1, K4, M1, K3. (12 sts)
Rnds 22–23: K all sts.
Rnd 24: K8, w&t, P4, w&t, K5, w&t, P6, w&t, K9.

Cut yarn, thread through live sts, and pull closed; use loose end to seam hole at bottom of paw. Stuff closed half of leg only. Seam unstuffed half to bottom of cat about 3–4 sts apart.

Cook came to work for the Morgans shortly after they were married. She knows all the food likes and dislikes of every person in the household, as well as most of the guests who come to visit—she remembers which one of them won't eat meat and who is intolerant of dairy. Unbeknownst to Mr. Morgan and at the request of his wife, Cook stirs a raw egg yolk into his nutty porridge every morning, which Mrs. Morgan read in an issue of the *Family Friend* magazine will provide her husband with extra energy for the day.

When anyone asks Cook about the cat that hangs around the kitchen, she scoffs and says to get it out of here, although the minute they leave she lets the cat back inside and gives her a saucer of milk. Cook has long, mumbled conversations with her cat late at night while prepping the next day's meals.

Cook's Cat

FINISHED SIZE
- 7.5 in./19 cm tall
- 12 in./30.5 cm long (not including tail)
- 6 in./15.25 cm wide

YARN
Cascade Aereo: 180 yd./164.5 m total (color A: 160 yd./146.25 m; color B [optional—belly color on black cat]: 20 yd./18.25 m)
- Black cat: 02 Charcoal (A) and 04 Ecru (B)
- Light gray cat: 03 Silver
- Calico cat: 04 Ecru (A), 02 Charcoal, and 17 Province

Note: The calico cat was made using intarsia in random spots across upper legs, back, and tail.

NEEDLES
- US size 5/3.75 mm double-pointed needles
- US size 5/3.75 mm straight needles

INSTRUCTIONS

Right Front Leg

Work begins at top/center of upper legs. With color A, CO 18 sts provisionally onto 1 dpn. The top of the leg is worked flat. Work 30 rows of stockinette stitch, beginning with a purl row.

Arrange sts on 3 dpns and join in the round.

Rnds 1–2: K all sts.
Row 3: K6, turn work.
Row 4: Slip 1, P7, turn work.
Row 5: Slip 1, K7.

Arrange these 8 sts onto 2 dpns. With RS together, work a 3-needle bind-off. Turn work right side out. Sts are now picked up around top edge of the cup-shape that was just created to begin the bottom of

the leg. Begin at the edge at the bind-off seam and PU/knit the following sts with 3 dpns:

1st dpn: PU 4 sts, K2 of the live sts.
2nd dpn: K6 of the live sts.
3rd dpn: K2 of the live sts, PU 4 (EOR). (18 sts)

Join sts in the round.

Rnd 1: K all sts.
Rnd 2: K2tog, K14, SSK. (16 sts)
Rnds 3–4: K all sts.
Rnd 5: K2tog, K12, SSK. (14 sts)
Rnds 6–8: K all sts.
Rnd 9: K2tog, K10, SSK. (12 sts)
Rnds 10–13: K all sts.
Rnd 14: K2tog, K8, SSK. (10 sts)
Rnds 15–19: K all sts.
Rnd 20: K3, (M1, K1) 5 times, K2. (15 sts)
Rnd 21: K all sts.
Rnd 22: K9, w&t, P3, w&t, K4, w&t, P5, w&t, K10.

Cut yarn, thread through live sts, and pull closed. Use loose end to seam hole at bottom of paw closed.

Left Front Leg

Unravel the scrap yarn that was used to cast on provisionally and place the 18 live sts onto 1 dpn. With WS facing, rejoin color A at first st and work 30 rows of flat stockinette stitch, beginning with a purl row.

Arrange sts on 3 dpns and join in the round.

Rnds 1–2: K all sts.
Row 3: K2, turn work.
Row 4: Slip 1, P7, turn work.
Row 5: Slip 1, K7.

Arrange these 8 sts onto 2 dpns. With RS together, work a 3-needle bind-off. Turn work right side out. Work the joint and the remainder of the leg the same as the right.

Body

Sts are now picked up around the back edge of the upper legs to begin the body, which is worked flat in stockinette stitch.

Setup: With RS of work facing, begin at the joint on the left leg, and with 1 straight needle and color A, PU 24 sts along the edge up to the top/center where the 2 legs were joined. This is about 3 sts for every 4 rows. Then PU 24 more sts with the same needle along the opposite edge, down to the right leg joint.

Row 1: P all sts.
Row 2: K all sts.
Row 3: P all sts.
Row 4: K24, place a stitch marker.

The curve in the cat's back is created with 5 sets of short rows that will begin and end at the stitch marker. Each set is followed by 3 rows of stockinette stitch (Rows 11–13).

Row 5: K12, w&t, P24, w&t, K12.
Row 6: K14, w&t, P28, w&t, K14.
Row 7: K16, w&t, P32, w&t, K16.
Row 8: K18, w&t, P36, w&t, K18.
Row 9: K20, w&t, P40, w&t, K20.
Row 10: K22, w&t, P44, w&t, K46 (to original EOR).
Row 11: P all sts.
Row 12: K all sts.
Row 13: P all sts.

Repeat Rows 4–13 four more times for a total of 5 sets of short rows. Then work the final 3 rows below.

Row 1: K22, place next 4 sts on a piece of scrap yarn, CO 4 new sts to working needle, K22.
Row 2: P all sts.
Row 3: K all sts.

Cut yarn; set work aside. Live sts can be left on needle or placed on scrap yarn.

Head

Sts are now picked up around the front edge of the upper legs to work the head, which is worked in the round on 3 dpns.

Setup: Begin at the top/center where the two upper legs were joined. With RS facing, pick up or CO the following sts with 3 dpns.

1st dpn: PU 17 sts in the first 21 rows of left leg.
2nd dpn: CO 4 sts onto dpn.
3rd dpn: Fold work so that WS are facing each other, PU 17 sts in last 21 rows of the right leg, opposite those that were picked up on the left leg (EOR). (38 sts)

Join sts in the round. **Note:** Stitches should be rearranged on the dpns for more even distribution after the first round.

Rnds 1–4: K all sts.
Rnd 5: K7, (M1, K2) 4 times, K1, SSK, K2, K2tog, K1, (K2, M1) 4 times, K7. (44 sts)
Rnd 6: K all sts.
Rnd 7: K7, (M1, K2) 6 times, SSK, K2, K2tog, (K2, M1) 6 times, K7. (54 sts)
Rnds 8–10: K all sts.
Rnd 11: (K2tog, K4) 9 times. (45 sts)
Rnds 12–13: K all sts.
Rnd 14: (K2tog, K3) 9 times. (36 sts)
Rnds 15–16: K all sts.
Rnd 17: (K2tog, K2) 9 times. (27 sts)
Rnds 18–19: K all sts.
Rnd 20: K2, SSK, K2tog, K15, SSK, K2tog, K2. (23 sts)
Rnd 21: K all sts.
Rnd 22: K1, SSK, K2tog, K13, SSK, K2tog, K1. (19 sts)
Rnd 23: K all sts.
Rnd 24: SSK, K2tog, K11, SSK, K2tog. (15 sts)
Rnd 25: K all sts.
Rnd 26: K2tog, K11, SSK. (13 sts)

Cut yarn, thread through remaining live sts, and pull closed.

Belly

The belly is worked flat with 2 dpns. It can be knit with color A or a second color (B). With RS facing, PU 4 sts in the 4 sts that were cast on between the legs.

Rows 1–17: Beginning with a purl row, work 17 rows of stockinette st.
Row 18: K1, M1L, K to 1 st before EOR, M1R, K1. (6 sts)
Row 19: P all sts.

Repeat Rows 18 and 19 until 24 sts, and then work 11 rows stockinette st. Cut yarn. Sides are left open at this time.

Base

Arrange the 48 body sts onto 2 dpns; join in the round with the 24 belly sts on a third dpn. (72 sts) Base is worked with color A. The EOR is at the end of the color A sts, but since sts are decreased evenly, it can be anywhere.

Rnd 1: K all sts.
Rnd 2: (K2tog, K4) 12 times. (60 sts)

Rnd 3: K all sts.
Rnd 4: (K2tog, K3) 12 times. (48 sts)
Rnd 5: K all sts.
Rnd 6: (K2tog, K2) 12 times. (36 sts)
Rnd 7: K all sts.
Rnd 8: (K2tog, K1) 12 times. (24 sts)
Rnd 9: K all sts.
Rnd 10: (K2tog) 12 times. (12 sts)

Cut yarn, thread through remaining live sts, and pull closed.

Tail

Place 4 sts from scrap yarn onto 1 dpn. Beginning at the bottom/center of the opening beneath the 4 live sts, pick up/knit the following sts along the edge of the opening with 3 dpns:

1st dpn: PU 6 sts from bottom/center of opening up to live sts.
2nd dpn: K4 live sts.
3rd dpn: PU 6 sts from live sts down to bottom/center of opening (EOR). (16 sts)

Join in the round.

Rnds 1–20: K all sts.
Rnd 21: K2tog, K12, SSK. (14 sts)
Rnds 22–41: K all sts.
Rnd 42: K2tog, K10, SSK. (12 sts)
Rnds 43–52: K all sts.

Cut yarn, thread through remaining live sts, and pull closed.

Stuff the tail, head, and front legs. The edges of the body and belly are now seamed together with whipstitch. This can be done with either color A or color B yarn. Seam all of one side and half of the other side. Finish stuffing body. Complete side seam.

Ears (make 2 the same)

The ears are worked separately and seamed to head. Work begins at bottom of ear. CO 15 sts onto 3 dpns; join in the round.

Rnds 1–2: K all sts.
Rnd 3: K1, SSK, K2tog, K5, SSK, K2tog, K1. (11 sts)
Rnds 4–5: K all sts.
Rnd 6: SSK, K2tog, K3, SSK, K2tog. (7 sts)
Rnds 7–8: K all sts.

Cut yarn, thread through remaining live sts, pull closed. Flatten ears with the CO tail coming from one bottom corner. Bend slightly to create a slight hollowing in the front and seam to head with about 5 sts between the inside corner of each ear.

Back Feet (make 2 the same)

The back feet are worked separately and seamed to the base. CO 12 sts onto 3 dpns and join in the round. K 12 rounds, and then cut yarn and thread through live sts. Pull closed. Stuff loosely and seam to flattened base about 10 rows apart from each other and with about ¾ in./2 cm sticking out in the front.

Designers of homes in the Victorian period were aware of the potential health hazards caused by indoor air, so in the latter part of the century many large homes for the upper class were built with porches in an array of styles. The Morgan family's porch is on the back side of their house, and the air is not only cleaner here but also cooler. Many an eventide is whiled away playing draughts and competing for the title of family champion.

The cat that spends her time on the porch looks forward to the family joining her. She is social and friendly and will take turns jumping from lap to lap in search of a head-scratch. She's learned to stay clear of the rocking chair, though, since one time she nearly lost her tail when the rockers rolled over it. After that, she developed the habit of holding her tail above her body whenever she lies down or goes into a full-length stretch.

The Porch Cat

FINISHED SIZE
- 17 in./43.25 cm long (not including tail)
- 9 in./22.75 cm tall
- 5 in./12.75 cm wide

YARN
Woolfolk Luft: 250 yd./228.5 m total
- Orange cat: Color L19
- Gray cat: Color L17
- Pale gray cat: Color L23

NEEDLES
- US size 5/3.75 mm double-pointed needles

INSTRUCTIONS

Front Legs (make 2 the same)

Work begins at top of each leg. CO 20 sts provisionally onto 1 dpn; these sts will flow directly into the body once the legs are finished.

Work 24 rows of stockinette stitch, beginning with a purl row and ending with a knit row; then arrange sts on 3 dpns and join in the round to knit the lower leg.

Rnds 1–2: K all sts.
Rnd 3: K2tog, K16, SSK. (18 sts)
Rnds 4–5: K all sts.
Rnd 6: K2tog, K14, SSK. (16 sts)
Rnds 7–8: K all sts.
Rnd 9: K2tog, K12, SSK. (14 sts)
Rnds 10–11: K all sts.
Rnd 12: K2tog, K10, SSK. (12 sts)
Rnds 13–22: K all sts.
Rnd 23: K2tog, K8, SSK. (10 sts)
Rnds 24–31: K all sts.
Rnd 32: K3, M1, K4, M1, K3. (12 sts)
Rnds 33–34: K all sts.
Rnd 35: (K4, M1) 2 times, K4. (14 sts)
Rnds 36–37: K all sts.

Cut yarn, thread through live sts, and pull closed.

Joining Two Legs in the Round

1. Unravel the provisional sts of one leg from the scrap yarn, placing the live sts on a dpn. Repeat with second leg and a second dpn.
2. CO 4 sts to a third dpn, and then, with same needle and RS facing, K first 12 sts of one of the legs.
3. With another dpn, K remaining 8 sts, plus the first 8 sts of the second leg.
4. With another dpn, K remaining 12 sts of second leg.
5. Finally, CO 4 new sts to end of this needle (EOR).

There are now a total of 48 sts with 16 sts on each dpn. The EOR is in the middle of the 8 new sts.

Join sts in the round to begin the body. The EOR is at the top/center of the body; the seams of the lower legs will run along the center/inside of each one.

Body

Rnds 1–10: K all sts.
Row 11: K24, place a stitch marker.

The following section contains short rows to shape the underside of the cat and change the direction of the sts to point upward. Each row in this section only will begin and end at the stitch marker. Knitting in the round resumes in Rnd 22.

Row 12: K4, w&t, P8, w&t, K4.
Row 13: K6, w&t, P12, w&t, K6.
Row 14: K8, w&t, P16, w&t, K8.
Row 15: K10, w&t, P20, w&t, K10.
Row 16: K12, w&t, P24, w&t, K12.
Row 17: K14, w&t, P28, w&t, K14.
Row 18: K16, w&t, P32, w&t, K16.
Row 19: K18, w&t, P36, w&t, K18.
Row 20: K20, w&t, P40, w&t, K20.
Row 21: K22, w&t, P44, w&t, K22, remove marker, K24 (to original EOR).
Rnds 22–36: K all sts.
Rnd 37: K1, M1R, K46, M1L, K1. (50 sts)

Rnds 38–42: K all sts.
Rnd 43: K1, M1R, K48, M1L, K1. (52 sts)
Rnds 44–48: K all sts.
Rnd 49: K1, M1R, K50, M1L, K1. (54 sts)
Rnds 50–54: K all sts.

Rows 55–64 are short rows to curve the back downward. Each of these begin and end at the EOR. The live sts that are set aside in Row 60 are for the tail. Knitting in the round resumes in Rnd 65.

Row 55: K4, w&t, P8, w&t, K4.
Row 56: K6, w&t, P12, w&t, K6.
Row 57: K8, w&t, P16, w&t, K8.
Row 58: K10, w&t, P20, w&t, K10.
Row 59: K12, w&t, P24, w&t, K12.
Row 60: K14, w&t, P28, w&t, K12, place last 2 sts in row plus first 2 sts of next row on a small piece of scrap yarn. CO 2 new sts to EOR.
Row 61: CO 2 new sts to working needle, K14, w&t, P32, w&t, K16.
Row 62: K18, w&t, P36, w&t, K18.
Row 63: K20, w&t, P40, w&t, K20.

Row 64: K22, w&t, P44, w&t, K22.
Rnd 65: K all sts.

Cut yarn; place live sts on scrap yarn.

The upper legs are now seamed together on the bottom of the cat. Keep in mind that the tail is at the top of your cat. Begin at the first row of the legs on the bottom and seam them together until you reach the point where the legs are joined in the round. The opening that remains between this point and the body is where the head will be.

Head

Sts are now picked up along the edges of the upper legs and front of body to begin the head. With RS facing, begin in the center of the 8 CO sts that were cast on between the legs. With 1 or 2 dpns, PU 26 sts down to the center point between the legs. With another 1 or 2 dpns, PU 26 sts along the opposite edge (EOR). (52 sts) Join in the round.

Rnd 1: K all sts.

The following section contains short rows to shape the head. Each one will begin and end at the EOR. Knitting in the round resumes in Rnd 9.

Row 2: K2, w&t, P4, w&t, K2.
Row 3: K5, w&t, P10, w&t, K5.
Row 4: K8, w&t, P16, w&t, K8.
Row 5: K11, w&t, P22, w&t, K11.
Row 6: K14, w&t, P28, w&t, K14.
Row 7: K17, w&t, P34, w&t, K17.
Row 8: K20, w&t, P40, w&t, K20.
Rnd 9: K23, SSK, K2, K2tog, K23. (50 sts)
Rnd 10: K all sts.
Rnd 11: K5, SSK, K2tog, K13, SSK, K2, K2tog, K13, SSK, K2tog, K5. (44 sts)
Rnd 12: K all sts.
Rnd 13: K4, SSK, K2tog, K11, SSK, K2, K2tog, K11, SSK, K2tog, K4. (38 sts)
Rnd 14: K all sts.
Rnd 15: K3, SSK, K2tog, K24, SSK, K2tog, K3. (34 sts)
Rnd 16: K all sts.
Rnd 17: K2, SSK, K2tog, K22, SSK, K2tog, K2. (30 sts)
Rnd 18: K all sts.
Rnd 19: K1, SSK, K2tog, K20, SSK, K2tog, K1. (26 sts)
Rnd 20: K all sts.
Rnd 21: SSK, K2tog, K18, SSK, K2tog. (22 sts)
Rnd 22: K all sts.
Rnd 23: K1, (K2tog) 10 times, K1. (12 sts)

Cut yarn, thread through remaining live sts, and pull closed.

Tail

Sts are now picked up around the edge of the opening beneath the 4 live sts to create the tail. Place the 4 live sts from scrap yarn onto a dpn. With RS facing, begin at the bottom/center of the opening and PU and/or knit the following sts with 3 dpns.

1st dpn: PU 5 sts along the edge from bottom/center to the first live st.
2nd dpn: K4 live sts.
3rd dpn: PU 5 along the opposite edge down to the bottom/center of opening (EOR). (14 sts total)

Join in the round.

Rnds 1–12: K all sts.
Rnd 13: K2tog, K10, SSK. (12 sts)
Rnds 14–28: K all sts.
Rnd 29: K2tog, K8, SSK. (10 sts)
Rnds 30–70: K all sts.

Cut yarn, thread through live sts, and pull closed.

Stuff front legs, head, chest, and tail. Leave the bulk of the body unstuffed while working the end of the body.

End of Body

Place the 54 live body sts back onto 3 dpns; join in the round.

Rnd 1: (K2tog, K4) 9 times. (45 sts)
Rnd 2: K all sts.
Rnd 3: (K2tog, K3) 9 times. (36 sts)
Rnd 4: K all sts.
Rnd 5: (K2tog, K2) 9 times. (27 sts)
Rnd 6: K all sts.
Rnd 7: (K2tog, K1) 9 times. (18 sts)
Rnd 8: K all sts.

Finish stuffing now before working the final round.

Rnd 9: (K2tog) 9 times. (9 sts)

Cut yarn, thread through remaining live sts, and pull closed.

Back Legs (make 2 the same)

The back legs are worked separately and seamed onto the body. CO 9 sts onto 3 dpns, join in the round.

Rnd 1: K all sts.
Rnd 2: (M1, K1) 9 times. (18 sts)
Rnd 3: K all sts.
Rnd 4: (M1, K2) 9 times. (27 sts)
Rnd 5: K all sts.
Rnd 6: (M1, K3) 9 times. (36 sts)
Rnds 7–16: K all sts.
Rnd 17: K1, K2tog, K30, SSK, K1. (34 sts)
Rnds 18–19: K all sts.
Rnd 20: K1, K2tog, K28, SSK, K1. (32 sts)
Rnds 21–22: K all sts.
Rnd 23: K1, K2tog, K26, SSK, K1. (30 sts)
Rnds 24–25: K all sts.
Rnd 26: K1, K2tog, K24, SSK, K1. (28 sts)
Rnds 27–28: K all sts.
Rnd 29: K1, K2tog, K22, SSK, K1. (26 sts)
Rnds 30–31: K all sts.
Rnd 32: K1, K2tog, K20, SSK, K1. (24 sts)

Rnds 33–34: K all sts.
Rnd 35: K1, K2tog, K18, SSK, K1. (22 sts)
Rnds 36–37: K all sts.
Rnd 38: K1, K2tog, K16, SSK, K1. (20 sts)
Rnds 39–40: K all sts.
Rnd 41: K1, K2tog, K14, SSK, K1. (18 sts)
Rnds 42–43: K all sts.
Rnd 44: K1, K2tog, K12, SSK, K1. (16 sts)
Rnds 45–46: K all sts.
Rnd 47: K1, K2tog, K10, SSK, K1. (14 sts)
Rnds 48–49: K all sts.
Row 50: K4, turn work.
Row 51: Slip 1, P7, turn work.
Row 52: Slip 1, K7.

Arrange the 8 sts just worked onto 2 dpns. Place RS together and work a 3-needle bind-off. Turn work right side out.

Sts are now picked up around the opening that was just created to begin the bottom of the leg. Beginning at the bind-off seam, pick up and knit the following 16 sts:

1st dpn: PU 5 sts along top edge from bind-off seam to live sts.
2nd dpn: K 6 live sts.
3rd dpn: PU 5 sts along top edge from live sts to the bind-off seam (EOR). (16 sts total) Join in the round.

Rnd 1: K all sts.
Rnd 2: K2tog, K12, SSK. (14 sts)
Rnd 3: K all sts.
Rnd 4: K2tog, K10, SSK. (12 sts)
Rnd 5: K all sts.
Rnd 6: K2tog, K8, SSK. (10 sts)
Rnds 7–20: K all sts.
Rnd 21: (K2, M1) 4 times, K2. (14 sts)
Rnds 22–25: K all sts.
Rnd 26: K9, w&t, P4, w&t, K5, w&t, P6, w&t, K10.

Stuff leg while still on the needles. Stuff the upper part loosely—it should be more flat than round; stuff bottom leg moderately. Cut yarn, thread through live sts, and pull closed. Use loose end to seam small hole at bottom of paw closed.

Hold both back legs on your cat as pictured, with top of each one 2 to 4 sts from the tail and pointing straight down (when the cat is in position, it will appear as if they are angled slightly backwards). While holding in place, set cat in its final stretched position so that you can see exactly where the legs should be, and then, with dpns or similar tools, attach them temporarily into this position, making sure they match each other. Finally, seam into place the portion of the upper legs that touch the body, about ½ in./1.25 cm inside the edge to keep it from showing.

Your Porch Cat may also require dpns or other support sticks inserted inside the back legs in order for them to stand straight.

Ears (make 2 the same)

The ears are worked separately and seamed to head. Work begins at bottom of ear. With color A, CO 15 sts onto 3 dpns; join in the round.

Rnds 1–2: K all sts.
Rnd 3: K1, SSK, K2tog, K5, SSK, K2tog, K1. (11 sts)
Rnds 4–5: K all sts.
Rnd 6: SSK, K2tog, K3, SSK, K2tog. (7 sts)
Rnds 7–8: K all sts.

Cut yarn, thread through remaining live sts, pull closed. Flatten ears with the CO tail coming from one bottom corner. Bend slightly to create a slight hollowing in the front and seam to head at the first decrease on each side.

Gertrude Morgan, at eight years old, likes making mud pies, rolling hoops, or playing kick the can with her twin brother, Timmy, as much as she enjoys dressing up in her mother's jewelry or helping Cook make biscuits. She is amiable and good natured and gets along with Aunt Pru better than anyone else in the house.

It was Trudy's idea to start a toy collection for the children of less privileged families last Christmas, donating a brand-new game she had just gotten for her birthday, one that she had been pining for for months.

Miss Trudy's only transgression (if you can call it that) is directed toward her tortoiseshell cat. Not that she means to torture the poor thing—she just doesn't realize what being dressed up in baby clothes and forced to attend tea parties alongside a myriad of dolls and stuffed animals does to a cat's self-esteem.

Miss Trudy's
Tortie

FINISHED SIZE

- 11 in./28 cm tall
- 4.5 in./11.5 cm wide
- 8 in./20.25 cm long (not including tail)

YARN

Note: The tortoiseshell effect is achieved by using 3 strands of very thin, furry yarn held together throughout the entire pattern: 2 strands of color A (primary color) and 1 strand of color B. The yarn called for in this pattern is labeled as Aran weight, but when knitted for a stuffed animal, it becomes barely fingering weight. In this pattern, 3 strands held together is equivalent to a heavier worsted weight.

Gedifra Laura: 495 yd./452.5 m total (color A, held double: 330 yd./302 m; color B, 1 strand: 165 yd./151 m)

- Cat 1: 2 strands of 03214 (A: orange) and 1 strand of 03207 (B: black) held together
- Cat 2: 2 strands of 03207 (A: black) and 1 strand of 03214 (B: orange) held together

NEEDLES

- US size 5/3.75 mm straight needles
- US size 5/3.75 mm double-pointed needles

INSTRUCTIONS

Chest

Work begins at neckline. The chest is worked flat. CO 36 sts onto 1 straight needle. Work a total of 29 rows in stockinette stitch, beginning and ending with a purl row.

Right Leg

K18, place remaining 18 sts on scrap yarn. Arrange the 18 just knitted sts onto 3 dpns; join in the round. Rows 2–5 are short rows to shape the back of the "elbow." Turn work after each.

Rnd 1: K all sts.
Row 2: K7, turn work.
Row 3: Slip 1, P7, turn work.
Row 4: Slip 1, K7, turn work.
Row 5: Slip 1, P7.

Arrange these 8 sts onto 2 dpns, 4 on each, and turn RS facing each other. Work a 3-needle bind-off. Cut yarn and pull through last st. Turn work right side out. This will make a sort of pocket in order to change the direction of the stitches and create the bend or joint in the leg.

Rejoin yarn at the bind-off seam (bottom/center of opening), and PU or knit the following sts with 3 dpns:

1st dpn: PU 4 from bottom/center of opening along the edge up to live sts, K2.
2nd dpn: K6 of the live sts.
3rd dpn: K2, PU 4 from live sts down to bottom/center of opening. (18 sts)

Rnds 1–3: K all sts.
Rnd 4: K2tog, K14, SSK. (16 sts)
Rnds 5–9: K all sts.
Rnd 10: K2tog, K12, SSK. (14 sts)
Rnds 11–15: K all sts.
Rnd 16: K2tog, K10, SSK. (12 sts)
Rnds 17–24: K all sts.
Rnd 25: K5, (M1, K1) 3 times, K4. (15 sts)
Rnds 26–27: K all sts.
Rnd 28: K10, w&t, P5, w&t, K6, w&t, P7, w&t, K11.

Cut yarn, thread through live sts, and pull closed. Use loose end to seam hole closed at bottom of paw.

Left Leg

Place 18 sts from scrap yarn onto 1 dpn. With RS facing, rejoin yarn at first st, K18. Arrange sts onto 3 dpns; join in the round. Rows 2–5 are short rows to shape the back of the "elbow." Turn work after each one of them.

Rnd 1: K all sts.
Row 2: K1, turn work.
Row 3: Slip 1, P7, turn work.
Row 4: Slip 1, K7, turn work.
Row 5: Slip 1, P7.

Work all elbow and leg instructions the same as for the right one.

Body

Setup: Hold first and last CO sts together and seam top 3 rows together, forming a circle that will serve as the neck opening. Beginning at the top/center of that circle (just below the seam), and with RS facing, rejoin yarn and PU the following sts along the edge of the chest with 3 dpns:

1st dpn: PU 28 sts along the right edge from top/center down to the right elbow (about 1 st for every 1 row).
2nd dpn: PU 12 sts along the edge from the right elbow across to the left elbow.
3rd dpn: PU 28 sts along the left edge from left elbow up to the top/center (about 1 st for every 1 row). (68 sts)

Rnd 1: K all sts.
Rnd 2: (K2tog) 2 times, K60, (SSK) 2 times. (64 sts)
Rnd 3: K all sts.
Rnd 4: (K2tog) 2 times, K56, (SSK) 2 times. (60 sts)
Rnd 5: K all sts.
Rnd 6: (K2tog) 2 times, K52, (SSK) 2 times. (56 sts)
Rnd 7: K all sts.
Rnd 8: (K2tog) 2 times, K48, (SSK) 2 times. (52 sts)
Rnds 9–13: K all sts.

Short rows are now worked to change the direction of the sts and curve the back downward. Each of these rows below has 2 short rows within it—one on the knit side of the fabric and one on the purl side—and each one begins and ends at the EOR. Knitting in the round resumes in Rnd 31.

Row 14: K4, w&t, P8, w&t, K4.
Row 15: K5, w&t, P10, w&t, K5.
Row 16: K6, w&t, P12, w&t, K6.
Row 17: K7, w&t, P14, w&t, K7.
Row 18: K8, w&t, P16, w&t, K8.
Row 19: K9, w&t, P18, w&t, K9.
Row 20: K10, w&t, P20, w&t, K10.
Row 21: K11, w&t, P22, w&t, K11.
Row 22: K12, w&t, P24, w&t, K12.
Row 23: K13, w&t, P26, w&t, K13.
Row 24: K14, w&t, P28, w&t, K14.
Row 25: K15, w&t, P30, w&t, K15.
Row 26: K16, w&t, P32, w&t, K16.
Row 27: K17, w&t, P34, w&t, K17.

Row 28: K18, w&t, P36, w&t, K18.
Row 29: K19, w&t, P38, w&t, K19.
Row 30: K20, w&t, P40, w&t, K20.
Rnds 31–46: K all sts.

Cut yarn. Place all sts on a piece of scrap yarn while the head is being worked.

Head

Sts are now picked up around the neck opening to work the head. Rejoin yarn where first and last CO sts were seamed together and PU 36 sts, 1 in each of the original CO sts. Join sts in the round.

Rnd 1: K all sts.
Rnd 2: K6, (M1, K1) 6 times, K4, SSK, K2tog, K4, (K1, M1) 6 times, K6. (46 sts)
Rnd 3: K all sts.
Row 4: K4, w&t, P8, w&t, K4.
Row 5: K6, w&t, P12, w&t, K6.
Row 6: K8, w&t, P16, w&t, K8.
Row 7: K10, w&t, P20, w&t, K10.
Row 8: K12, w&t, P24, w&t, K12.
Row 9: K14, w&t, P28, w&t, K14.
Row 10: K16, w&t, P32, w&t, K16.
Row 11: K18, w&t, P36, w&t, K18.
Row 12: K20, w&t, P40, w&t, K20.
Rnd 13: K4, SSK, K2tog, K13, SSK, K2tog, K13, SSK, K2tog, K4. (40 sts)
Rnd 14: K all sts.
Rnd 15: K3, SSK, K2tog, K26, SSK, K2tog, K3. (36 sts)

Rnd 16: K all sts.
Rnd 17: K2, SSK, K2tog, K24, SSK, K2tog, K2. (32 sts)
Rnd 18: K all sts.
Rnd 19: K1, SSK, K2tog, K22, SSK, K2tog, K1. (28 sts)
Rnd 20: K all sts.
Rnd 21: SSK, K2tog, K20, SSK, K2tog. (24 sts)
Rnd 22: K all sts.
Rnd 23: (SSK) 6 times, (K2tog) 6 times. (12 sts)
Rnd 24: K all sts.
Rnd 25: (SSK) 3 times, (K2tog) 3 times. (6 sts)

Cut yarn, thread through remaining live sts, and pull closed.

Stuff head and front legs now before working the base. Do not stuff the body yet.

Base

Place 52 sts from scrap yarn back onto dpns. Rejoin yarn at first st.

Rnd 1: K49, place last 3 sts in rnd plus first 3 sts from next rnd onto a piece of scrap yarn, CO 3 new sts to EOR.
Rnd 2: CO 3 new sts to working needle, K49. (52 sts)
Rnd 3: K all sts.
Rnd 4: (K2, K2tog) 13 times. (39 sts)
Rnd 5: K all sts.
Rnd 6: (K1, K2tog) 13 times. (26 sts)
Rnd 7: K all sts.

Finish stuffing the rest of the body fully now. Use a dpn from the outside to shift stuffing forward.

Rnd 8: (K2tog) 13 times. (13 sts)
Rnds 9–10: K all sts.

Cut yarn, thread through remaining live sts, and pull closed. Weave in loose end. Base is flattened to provide firm seating.

Tail

Setup: Place 6 live sts from scrap yarn onto a dpn. With RS facing, begin at the bottom/center of the opening beneath the live sts and pick up/knit 18 sts as follows:

1st dpn: PU 6 sts along the left edge from bottom/ center of opening up to live sts.
2nd dpn: K6 live sts.
3rd dpn: PU 6 sts along the right edge from live sts down to bottom/center of opening.

Note: The tail will need to be stuffed (loosely) a little at a time as you proceed.

Rnds 1–5: K all sts.
Rnd 6: K2tog, K14, SSK. (16 sts)
Rnds 7–11: K all sts.
Rnd 12: K2tog, K12, SSK. (14 sts)
Rnds 13–17: K all sts.
Rnd 18: K2tog, K10, SSK. (12 sts)
Rnds 19–42: K all sts.
Rnd 43: K2tog, K8, SSK. (10 sts)
Rnds 44–45: K all sts.

Rnd 46: K2tog, K6, SSK. (8 sts)
Rnds 47–48: K all sts.

Cut yarn, thread through remaining live sts, and pull closed. Weave in loose end.

Ears (make 2 the same)

The ears are worked separately and seamed to head. Work begins at bottom of ear. CO 15 sts onto 3 dpns; join in the round.

Rnds 1–2: K all sts.
Rnd 3: K1, SSK, K2tog, K5, SSK, K2tog, K1. (11 sts)
Rnds 4–5: K all sts.
Rnd 6: SSK, K2tog, K3, SSK, K2tog. (7 sts)
Rnds 7–8: K all sts.

Cut yarn, thread through remaining live sts, pull closed. Flatten ears with the CO tail coming from one bottom corner. Bend slightly to create a slight hollowing in the front and seam to head at first decrease on each side, with about 5 sts between the inside corner of each ear.

Back Feet (make 2 the same)

The back feet are worked separately and seamed to the base. CO 12 sts onto 3 dpns and join in the round. K 13 rounds, and then cut yarn and thread through live sts. Pull closed. Stuff loosely and seam to flattened base side by side with 1 in./2.5 cm sticking out in the front.

Most large Victorian country homes had at least a small garden to grow herbs and vegetables for the family. The garden behind the Morgan house is a little overgrown and never quite the picture-perfect version that Mrs. Morgan sees in her magazine. Nevertheless, she loves to spend time there and does the best she can to take care of it since the gardener left.

There is a feral tomcat living in the garden. Mrs. Morgan has seen him standing on his back legs to swat bugs and butterflies. She lets him stay because he's good at keeping the rabbits out, much more of a deterrent to them than the scarecrow the twins put up last year.

Surrounding the garden is an old wooden fence with a little wooden gate, and that is where the woodbine twineth.

The
Garden
Cat

FINISHED SIZE
- 14 in./35.5 cm tall
- 6 in./15.25 cm wide
- 6 in./15.25 cm deep (not including tail)

YARN
Berroco Ultra Alpaca Chunky: 240 yd./219.5 m total
(color A: 190 yd./173.5 m; color B: 50 yd./45.5 m)
- Cat 1: 7292 Tiger's Eye Mix (A)
  and 7201 Winter White (B)
- Cat 2: 7289 Charcoal Mix (A) and
  7201 Winter White (B)
- Cat 3: 7207 Salt & Pepper (A)
  and 7206 Light Grey (B)

NEEDLES
- US size 5/3.75 mm straight needles
- US size 5/3.75 mm double-pointed needles

INSTRUCTIONS

Back

Work begins at neckline. Both back and belly pieces
are worked flat. With color A, CO 28 sts onto 1
straight needle. Purl all sts on Row 1 and every odd
row. Place a removable stitch marker on the first and
last sts of Rows 19 and 29 below.

Row 2: K all sts.
Row 4: K all sts.
Row 6: K all sts.
Row 8: K1, M1R, K26, M1L, K1. (30 sts)
Row 10: K all sts.
Row 12: K1, M1R, K28, M1L, K1. (32 sts)
Row 14: K all sts.
Row 16: K1, M1R, K30, M1L, K1. (34 sts)

Rows 17–29: Straight stockinette stitch.
Row 30: K9, (M1, K2) 8 times, K9. (42 sts)

The following row contains several short rows within
it to slightly curve the direction of the stitches.

Row 32: K29, w&t, P16, w&t, K20, w&t, P24, w&t,
  K28, w&t, P32, w&t, K37 (EOR).
Row 33–59: Straight stockinette stitch.
Row 60: K17, SSK, K4, K2tog, K17. (40 sts)
Row 62: K13, (SSK, K2) 2 times, (K2tog, K2) 2
  times, K11. (36 sts)
Row 64: K15, place 6 sts on scrap yarn, CO 6 new
  sts to working needle, K15.
Row 66: K all sts.

Do not cut yarn; set work aside.

Belly

Work begins at neckline. With color B, CO 12 sts
onto 1 straight needle or dpn. Purl all sts on Row 1
and every odd row. Place a removable stitch marker
on the first and last sts of Rows 19 and 29 below.

Row 2: K all sts.
Row 4: K all sts.
Row 6: K1, M1R, K10, M1L, K1. (14 sts)
Rows 7–15: Straight stockinette stitch.

Row 16: K1, M1R, K12, M1L, K1. (16 sts)
Rows 17–25: Straight stockinette stitch.
Row 26: K1, M1R, K14, M1L, K1. (18 sts)
Rows 27–66: Straight stockinette stitch.

Cut yarn; place all sts onto 1 dpn. Place 36 color A sts from the back onto 2 dpns and join in the round with color B sts. Work base.

Base

The base is worked in the round with dpns and color A yarn. (54 sts)

Rnd 1: (K2tog, K4) 9 times. (45 sts)
Rnd 2: K all sts.
Rnd 3: (K2tog, K3) 9 times. (36 sts)
Rnd 4: K all sts.
Rnd 5: (K2tog, K2) 9 times. (27 sts)
Rnd 6: K all sts.
Rnd 7: (K2tog, K1) 9 times. (18 sts)
Rnd 8: K all sts.
Rnd 9: (K2tog) 9 times. (9 sts)

Cut yarn, thread through remaining live sts, and pull closed.

The back and belly pieces are now seamed together. With WS together and using either color A or color B and a darning needle, begin at the base and seam edges together along one side up to the lower stitch marker. Cut yarn and secure loose end. Rejoin yarn at upper stitch marker and seam up to the neckline

of each piece. Cut yarn; secure end. On the other side, seam from neckline to upper stitch marker and about 1–2 in./2.5–5 cm below lower stitch marker only. This will leave an opening at the bottom for adding stuffing.

Head

Sts are now picked up in the original CO sts to begin the head.

Setup: With color A and RS facing, begin in the back/center of the neckline and PU the following number of sts with 3 dpns:

1st dpn: PU 14 sts from the back/center to the end of the color A sts.
2nd dpn: PU 12 sts across the color B sts in the front.
3rd dpn: PU 14 sts from the end of the color B sts to the back/center. (40 sts)

The head is worked with a combination of short rows, worked on both sides of the EOR, and knitting in the round.

Row 1: K10, w&t, P20, w&t, K10.
Row 2: K12, w&t, P24, w&t, K12.
Row 3: K2, (K2, M1) 6 times, K12, (M1, K2) 6 times, K2. (52 sts)
Rnds 4–10: K all sts.
Row 11: K5, SSK, K2tog, K5, w&t, P17, P2tog, SSP, P5, w&t, K12. (48 sts)
Row 12: K4, SSK, K2tog, K6, w&t, P16, P2tog, SSP, P6, w&t, K12. (44 sts)
Row 13: K3, SSK, K2tog, K7, w&t, P15, P2tog, SSP, P7, w&t, K12. (40 sts)
Row 14: K2, SSK, K2tog, K8, w&t, P14, P2tog, SSP, P8, w&t, K12. (36 sts)
Row 15: K1, SSK, K2tog, K9, w&t, P13, P2tog, SSP, P9, w&t, K12. (32 sts)
Row 16: K1, SSK, K2tog, K10, w&t, P14, P2tog, SSP, P10, w&t, K13. (28 sts)
Rnd 17: K all sts.
Rnd 18: K1, SSK, K2tog, K4, SSK, K2tog, K2, SSK, K2tog, K4, SSK, K2tog, K1. (20 sts)
Rnd 19: K all sts.

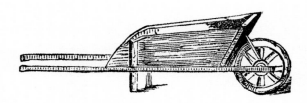

Rnd 20: K1, (SSK, K2tog) 2 times, K2, (SSK, K2tog) 2 times, K1. (12 sts)

Rnd 21: K all sts.

Rnd 22: K1, SSK, K2tog, K2, SSK, K2tog, K1. (8 sts)

Cut yarn, thread through remaining live sts, and pull closed.

Arms (make 2 the same)

Sts are now picked up around the openings at the sides of the body to work the arms.

Setup: With color A, begin at the bottom/center of one of the openings and pick up 20 sts evenly around the edges of the opening with 3 dpns (EOR).

Rnds 1–3: K all sts.

Rnd 4: K2tog, K16, SSK. (18 sts)

Rnds 5–7: K all sts.

Rnd 8: K2tog, K14, SSK. (16 sts)

Rnds 9–11: K all sts.

Rnd 12: K2tog, K12, SSK. (14 sts)

Rnds 13–15: K all sts.

Rnd 16: K2tog, K10, SSK. (12 sts)

Rnds 17–19: K all sts.

Several short rows are included within the following round that will bend the "wrist" downward:

Rnd 20: K11, w&t, P10, w&t, K8, w&t, P6, w&t, K9 (EOR).

Rnds 21–25: K all sts.

Rnd 26: (K4, M1) 2 times, K4. (14 sts)

Rnds 27–30: K all sts.

Cut yarn, thread through live sts, and pull closed. The arms are brought into desired position and either tacked in place with color A or hot-glued in place.

Tail

Sts are now picked up around the opening at the bottom/back of your cat to work the tail.

Setup: Place the 6 sts from scrap yarn onto 1 dpn. With color A, begin at the bottom/center of the opening and pick up or knit the following sts with 3 dpns:

1st dpn: PU 6 sts from bottom/center of opening up to the live sts.

2nd dpn: K6 live sts.

3rd dpn: PU 6 sts from live sts down to the bottom/center (EOR). (18 sts)

Rnds 1–10: K all sts.

Rnd 11: K2tog, K14, SSK. (16 sts)

Rnds 12–21: K all sts.

Rnd 22: K2tog, K12, SSK. (14 sts)

Rnds 23–52: K all sts.

Rnd 53: K2tog, K10, SSK. (12 sts)

Rnd 54: K all sts.

Rnd 55: K2tog, K8, SSK. (10 sts)

Rnd 56: K all sts.

Cut yarn, thread through remaining live sts, and pull closed.

Stuff all parts of your cat moderately now; finish side seam.

Ears (make 2 the same)

The ears are worked separately and seamed to the head. With color A, CO 15 sts onto 3 dpns; join in the round.

Rnds 1–2: K all sts.

Rnd 3: K2, SSK, K2tog, K3, SSK, K2tog, K2. (11 sts)

Rnds 4–5: K all sts.

Rnd 6: K1, SSK, K2tog, K1, SSK, K2tog, K1. (7 sts)

Rnds 7–8: K all sts.

Cut yarn, thread through remaining live sts, and pull closed. Weave in loose end. Use CO tail to seam to head.

Back Legs (make 2 the same)

The back legs are worked separately and then seamed to the sides of the body.

Setup: With color A, CO 10 sts onto 1 dpn. Multiple short rows are included in Row 2 of the setup to shape the top of the leg.

Row 1: P all sts.
Row 2: K7, w&t, P4, w&t, K5, w&t, P6, w&t, K7, w&t, P8, w&t, K9 (EOR).

Turn work so that the working yarn is coming from the top stitch. Sts are now picked up along the sides and CO edge of work. With RS facing and 2 additional dpns, pick up 1 st along the top edge, 8 sts in the original CO sts, and 1 st along the bottom edge for a total of 10 new sts (EOR). Knitting in the round begins. It's helpful to keep the original sts on the first dpn and the picked-up sts on the other 2 dpns in order to keep track of where the EOR is. (20 sts)

Rnd 1: K all sts.
Rnd 2: (M1, K10, M1L in the bar between sts) 2 times. (24 sts)
Rnd 3: K all sts.
Rnd 4: (M1, K12, M1L in the bar between sts) 2 times. (28 sts)
Rnds 5–16: K all sts.
Rnd 17: (K2tog, K10, SSK) 2 times. (24 sts)
Rnds 18–21: K all sts.

Rnd 22: (K2tog, K8, SSK) 2 times. (20 sts)
Rnds 23–26: K all sts.

The following short rows will shape the heel and are worked on both sides of the EOR. Knitting in the round resumes in Rnd 33.

Row 27: K1, w&t, P2, w&t, K1.
Row 28: K2, w&t, P4, w&t, K2.
Row 29: K3, w&t, P6, w&t, K3.
Row 30: K1, w&t, P2, w&t, K1.
Row 31: K2, w&t, P4, w&t, K2.
Row 32: K4, w&t, P8, w&t, K4.
Rnd 33: (K2tog, K6, SSK) 2 times. (16 sts)
Rnd 34: K all sts.
Rnd 35: (K2tog, K4, SSK) 2 times. (12 sts)
Rnds 36–45: K all sts.
Rnd 46: (K4, M1) 2 times, K4. (14 sts)
Rnd 47: K all sts.

The last round contains multiple short rows to shape the end of the foot:

Rnd 48: K9, w&t, P4, w&t, K5, w&t, P6, w&t, K7, w&t, P8, w&t, K11 (EOR).

Cut yarn and thread through live sts. Stuff moderately through opening; pull closed. The top (thigh) section of the back leg should be flattened after stuffing. Weave in loose end. Position back legs to side of body so that the cat is sitting up straight and the foot is flat on the ground and faces straight forward. Seam around all sides of thigh and back of foot. The front of the foot is left sticking out in front of the body.

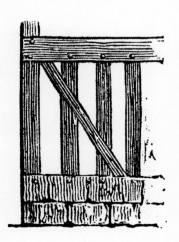

Large country homes in the nineteenth century often included a carriage house—a separate structure behind the main house designed to provide covered space for the family's vehicle. The Morgans' carriage house is two-storied with a double-sided front door that swings open and is broad enough for the family carriage to get in and out of easily.

The coachman and stable boy are housed in a loft on the top floor along with one of the quickest and most clever cats in the county—a mouser, which the men allow to stay because they're impressed with her skill and she requires no food or attention other than a quick scratch behind an ear when she brings them her prey.

The Carriage House Cat

FINISHED SIZE
• 14 in./35.5 cm long (not including tail)
• 7 in./18 cm wide

YARN
Berroco Ultra Alpaca Chunky Natural:
200 yd./183 m total
• Gray cat: 72512 Poppy Seed
• Cream cat: 72500 Jasmine Rice
• Light brown cat: 72511 Millet

NEEDLES
• US size 5/3.75 mm double-pointed needles

INSTRUCTIONS

Right Leg
Work begins at the top of the right leg, which will be the top/center of the back. CO 8 sts provisionally onto 1 dpn. The upper leg portions of both legs are worked flat.

Row 1: P all sts.
Row 2: K all sts.
Row 3: P all sts.
Row 4: K1, M1L, K7. (9 sts)
Row 5: P all sts.
Row 6: K all sts.
Row 7: P all sts.
Row 8: K1, M1L, K8. (10 sts)
Row 9: P all sts.
Row 10: K all sts.
Row 11: P all sts.
Row 12: K1, M1L, K9. (11 sts)
Row 13: P all sts.
Row 14: K all sts.
Row 15: P all sts.
Row 16: K1, M1L, K10. (12 sts)
Row 17: P all sts.

Row 18: K all sts.
Row 19: P all sts.
Row 20: K1, M1L, K11. (13 sts)
Row 21: P all sts.
Row 22: K all sts.
Row 23: P all sts.
Row 24: K1, M1L, K12. (14 sts)
Row 25: P all sts.
Row 26: K all sts.
Row 27: P all sts.
Row 28: K1, M1L, K13. (15 sts)
Row 29: P all sts.
Row 30: K all sts.
Row 31: P all sts.
Row 32: K1, M1L, K14. (16 sts)
Row 33: P all sts.
Row 34: Slip 1, K9, turn work.
Row 35: Slip 1, P9, turn work.
Row 36: Slip 1, K9, turn work.
Row 37: Slip 1, P9.

Arrange these 10 sts evenly onto 2 dpns, and with RS together work a 3-needle bind-off (place remaining 6 sts on a third dpn by themselves). Turn work RS out.

Sts are now picked up on each side of the bind-off seam to begin the bottom of the leg. Beginning at the bind-off seam, pick up and knit the following 18 sts:

1st dpn: PU 6 sts along top edge from bind-off seam to live sts.
2nd dpn: K6 live sts.
3rd dpn: PU 6 sts along top edge from last live st to the bind-off seam.

Join sts in the round.

Rnds 1–3: K all sts.
Rnd 4: K2tog, K14, SSK. (16 sts)
Rnds 5–7: K all sts.
Rnd 8: K2tog, K12, SSK. (14 sts)
Rnds 9–11: K all sts.
Rnd 12: K2tog, K10, SSK. (12 sts)
Rnds 13–15: K all sts.
Rnd 16: K2tog, K8, SSK. (10 sts)
Rnds 17–24: K all sts.
Rnd 25: (K2, M1) 4 times, K2. (14 sts)
Rnds 26–29: K all sts.
Rnd 30: K9, w&t, P4, w&t, K5, w&t, P6, w&t, K10.

Cut yarn, thread through live sts, and pull closed. Use loose end to seam small hole at bottom of paw.

Left Leg

Remove the scrap yarn from the provisional CO sts of the right leg, placing them onto a dpn. The left leg is worked directly from these 8 sts. With WS facing, rejoin working yarn at first st.

Row 1: P all sts.
Row 2: K all sts.
Row 3: P all sts.
Row 4: K7, M1R, K1. (9 sts)
Row 5: P all sts.
Row 6: K all sts.
Row 7: P all sts.
Row 8: K8, M1R, K1. (10 sts)
Row 9: P all sts.
Row 10: K all sts.
Row 11: P all sts.
Row 12: K9, M1R, K1. (11 sts)
Row 13: P all sts.
Row 14: K all sts.
Row 15: P all sts.
Row 16: K10, M1R, K1. (12 sts)
Row 17: P all sts.
Row 18: K all sts.
Row 19: P all sts.
Row 20: K11, M1R, K1. (13 sts)

Free mouse pattern is available at rabbitholeknits.com

1st dpn: PU 6 sts to the left of bind-off seam; join 6 live sts.

2nd dpn: K6 live sts.

3rd dpn: PU 6 sts from last live st to the bind-off seam.

Join sts in the round. Work the bottom of the left leg (Rnds 1–30) the same as the right leg.

Body

Setup: Sts are now picked up along the back edge of the upper legs to begin the body.

With RS facing, begin at the top/center where the 2 legs are joined, and pick up the following 60 sts with 4 dpns:

1st dpn: PU 15 sts in 15 rows from top/center down.

2nd dpn: PU the next 15 sts in the next 15 rows.

The knitter should now be where the right leg is joined in the round. Bring front legs together and pick up sts on the opposite leg:

Note: Although the front legs are brought together while picking up sts, they will end up being a few sts apart in the end; this result is natural and expected.

3rd dpn: PU 15 sts in 15 rows beginning at the bottom of the left upper leg.

4th dpn: PU the next 15 sts in 15 rows.

The knitter should now be back at the top/center where the 2 upper legs were joined. Join sts in the round.

Rnds 1–8: K all sts.
Rnd 9: K1, M1R, K58, M1L, K1. (62 sts)
Rnds 10–17: K all sts.
Rnd 18: K1, M1R, K60, M1L, K1. (64 sts)
Rnds 19–26: K all sts.
Rnd 27: K1, M1R, K62, M1L, K1. (66 sts)
Rnds 28–35: K all sts.
Rnd 36: K1, M1R, K64, M1L, K1. (68 sts)
Rnds 37–44: K all sts.
Rnd 45: K1, M1R, K66, M1L, K1. (70 sts)
Rnds 46–47: K all sts.
Row 48: K8, w&t, P16, w&t, K8.

Row 21: P all sts.
Row 22: K all sts.
Row 23: P all sts.
Row 24: K12, M1R, K1. (14 sts)
Row 25: P all sts.
Row 26: K all sts.
Row 27: P all sts.
Row 28: K13, M1R, K1. (15 sts)
Row 29: P all sts.
Row 30: K all sts.
Row 31: P all sts.
Row 32: K14, M1R, K1. (16 sts)
Row 33: P all sts.
Row 34: K all sts.
Row 35: Slip 1, P9, turn work.
Row 36: Slip 1, K9, turn work.
Row 37: Slip 1, P9, turn work.
Row 38: Slip 1, K9.

Arrange these 10 sts evenly onto 2 dpns, and with RS together work a 3-needle bind-off (place remaining 6 sts on a third dpn by themselves). Turn work RS out.

Sts are now picked up on each side of the bind-off seam to begin the bottom of the leg. Beginning at the bind-off seam, pick up and knit the following 18 sts:

Row 49: K10, w&t, P20, w&t, K10.
Row 50: K12, w&t, P24, w&t, K12.
Row 51: K14, w&t, P28, w&t, K14.
Row 52: K16, w&t, P32, w&t, K16.
Row 53: K18, w&t, P36, w&t, K18.
Row 54: K20, w&t, P40, w&t, K17, place last 3 sts in round, plus first 3 sts of next round onto small piece of scrap yarn, CO 3 new sts to EOR.
Row 55: CO 3 new sts to working needle, K19, w&t, P44, w&t, K22.
Row 56: K24, w&t, P48, w&t, K24.
Row 57: K26, w&t, P52, w&t, K26.
Row 58: K28, w&t, P56, w&t, K28.
Rnd 59: K all sts.

Place all sts on a piece of scrap yarn for working the end of body later. Cut yarn or, if a second ball is available to work the head and tail, roll working yarn into a ball and stick inside the body.

Positioning Steps

At this time, two important steps are taken in order to create the proper crouching position for your cat; a third positioning step is taken after the body is stuffed. Begin by stuffing the front legs.

1. Bridge between legs: A tiny bit of fabric is knit to join part of the 2 front legs from the elbows toward the paws. With RS facing, PU 4 sts along the edge of the body between the legs. Turn work, P all sts. Continue working in stockinette stitch for a total of 9 rows; bind off, leaving a tail of several inches for seaming. Ensuring that the leg decreases are centered

on the bottom, seam the sides of the bridge to the sides of the legs.

2. The last 8 rows of the upper (flat) section of each leg are brought down onto the center of the lower (round) section and seamed there from the outside.

Head

Stitches are now picked up around the front of the legs and across the bridge to begin the head.

Setup: With RS facing, begin at the top/center of work and with 3 dpns PU the following 56 sts:

1st dpn: PU 22 sts from top/center down to leg.
2nd dpn: PU 4 sts from leg to bridge, PU 4 sts across bind-off edge of bridge, and 4 sts across leg to the work on opposite side.
3rd dpn: PU 22 sts from leg to top/center.

Sts are joined in the round and may be rearranged on the needles after a few rounds.

Rnds 1–2: K all sts.
Rnd 3: (K2tog, K2) 14 times. (42 sts)
Rnds 4–11: K all sts.
Rnd 12: K8, (M1, K2) 4 times, K10, (K2, M1) 4 times, K8. (50 sts)
Row 13: K6, w&t, P12, w&t, K6.
Row 14: K8, w&t, P16, w&t, K8.
Row 15: K10, w&t, P20, w&t, K10.
Rnd 16: K4, SSK, K2tog, K13, SSK, K4, K2tog, K13, SSK, K2tog, K4. (44 sts)

Rnd 17: K all sts.

Rnd 18: K3, SSK, K2tog, K11, SSK, K4, K2tog, K11, SSK, K2tog, K3. (38 sts)

Rnd 19: K all sts.

Rnd 20: K2, SSK, K2tog, K9, SSK, K4, K2tog, K9, SSK, K2tog, K2. (32 sts)

Rnd 21: K all sts.

Rnd 22: K1, SSK, K2tog, K22, SSK, K2tog, K1. (28 sts)

Rnd 23: K all sts.

Rnd 24: SSK, K2tog, K20, SSK, K2tog. (24 sts)

Rnd 25: K all sts.

Rnd 26: (SSK) 6 times, (K2tog) 6 times. (12 sts)

Rnd 27: K all sts.

Rnd 28: (SSK) 3 times, (K2tog) 3 times. (6 sts)

Cut yarn, thread through remaining live sts, and pull closed.

Tail

Setup: Place 6 sts from scrap yarn onto 1 dpn. With RS facing, begin at the bottom/center of hole beneath live sts and PU/knit the following 18 sts to begin the tail:

1st dpn: PU 6 sts from bottom/center of hole to live sts.

2nd dpn: K6 live sts.

3rd dpn: PU 6 sts from live sts to bottom/center of hole.

Rnds 1–10: K all sts.

Rnd 11: K2tog, K14, SSK. (16 sts)

Rnds 12–21: K all sts.

Rnd 22: K2tog, K12, SSK. (14 sts)

Rnds 23–32: K all sts.

Rnd 33: K2tog, K10, SSK. (12 sts)

Rnds 34–53: K all sts.

Rnd 54: K2tog, K8, SSK. (10 sts)

Rnds 55–69: K all sts.

Cut yarn, thread through remaining live sts, and pull closed. Stuff head and tail now.

End of Body

Place the 70 live sts from scrap yarn back onto 4 dpns.

Rnd 1: (K2tog, K3) 14 times. (56 sts)

Rnd 2: K all sts.

Rnd 3: (K2tog, K2) 14 times. (42 sts)

Rnd 4: K all sts.

Rnd 5: (K2tog, K1) 14 times. (28 sts)

Rnd 6: K all sts.

Rnd 7: (K2tog) 14 times. (14 sts)

Rnd 8: K all sts.

Complete stuffing at this time. A dpn can be used from the outside to shift stuffing forward toward the head and evenly throughout the body. Make sure stuffing is sufficient to create the rise at the rear of your cat.

Rnd 9: (K2tog) 7 times. (7 sts)

Cut yarn, thread through remaining live sts, and pull closed.

Final Positioning Step

Hold the back of one of the front legs to the body and seam in place from the elbows upward about 2 in./5 cm. Repeat with the other leg.

Ears (make 2 the same)

The ears are worked separately and seamed to head. Work begins at bottom of ear. CO 15 sts onto 3 dpns; join in the round.

Rnds 1–2: K all sts.
Rnd 3: K1, SSK, K2tog, K5, SSK, K2tog, K1. (11 sts)
Rnds 4–5: K all sts.
Rnd 6: SSK, K2tog, K3, SSK, K2tog. (7 sts)
Rnds 7–8: K all sts.

Cut yarn, thread through remaining live sts, and pull closed. Flatten ears with the CO tail coming from one bottom corner. Bend slightly to create a slight hollowing in the front and seam to head 2 rows behind the first decrease on each side, with about 5 sts between them.

Back Legs (make 2 the same)

The back legs are worked separately and seamed to the bottom of your cat. CO 16 sts onto 3 dpns; join in the round.

Rnds 1–2: K all sts.
Row 3: K5, turn work.
Row 4: Slip 1, P9, turn work.
Row 5: Slip 1, K9, turn work.
Row 6: Slip 1, P9, turn work.
Row 7: Slip 1, K9.

Arrange these 10 sts evenly onto 2 dpns, and with RS together work a 3-needle bind-off (place remaining 6 sts on a third dpn by themselves). Turn work RS out.

Sts are now picked up on each side of the bind-off seam to begin the bottom of the leg. Beginning at the bind-off seam, pick up and knit the following 16 sts:

1st dpn: PU 5 sts along top edge from bind-off seam to live sts.
2nd dpn: K6 live sts.
3rd dpn: PU 5 sts along top edge from last live st to the bind-off seam.

Join sts in the round; continue with the bottom section of the back leg.

Rnd 1: K all sts. (16 sts)
Rnd 2: K2tog, K12, SSK. (14 sts)
Rnd 3: K all sts.
Rnd 4: K2tog, K10, SSK. (12 sts)
Rnd 5: K all sts.
Rnd 6: K2tog, K8, SSK. (10 sts)
Rnds 7–14: K all sts.
Rnd 15: (K2, M1) 4 times, K2. (14 sts)
Rnds 16–19: K all sts.
Rnd 20: K9, w&t, P4, w&t, K5, w&t, P6, w&t, K10.

Cut yarn, thread through live sts, and pull closed. Use loose end to seam small hole at bottom of paw.

Seam legs to bottom of cat in line with the front legs and about 5 sts apart from each other in the center. Add additional stuffing to the heel so that it's stiff just before seaming it closed.

Emily Morgan is fifteen years old. She is quiet, kind, and well mannered. She has an especially close relationship with her father and, like him, has shown a natural aptitude for mathematics. Twice he has taken her to his office to show her the ropes, as he calls it.

Emily has taken piano lessons since she was five and has become an accomplished pianist. She holds herself to a strict practice schedule and plays for guests in the parlour on Sundays. Timmy always requests "A Life on the Ocean Wave," which she happily plays for him—complete with all the trills.

The cat that belongs to Miss Morgan is a manx. He wandered up to the house one day, skinny and in great need; Emily was the first to see him and take him in. Researching the breed in the family's encyclopedia, she was very interested to learn that they originated on the Isle of Man and that their tail stumps can vary in length.

Miss
Morgan's
Manx

FINISHED SIZE
- 11 in./28 cm long
- 10 in./25.5 cm tall
- 4 in./10 cm wide

YARN
Berroco Ultra Alpaca Chunky: 150 yd./137 m total
- Cat 1: 7292 Tiger's Eye Mix
- Cat 2: 7289 Charcoal Mix
- Cat 3: 7201 Winter White

NEEDLES
- US size 5/3.75 mm straight needles
- US size 5/3.75 mm double-pointed needles

INSTRUCTIONS

Chest

Work begins at neckline. CO 36 sts onto 1 straight needle; work all rows flat.

Row 1: P all sts.
Row 2: K all sts.

Repeat Rows 1 and 2 eight more times for a total of 18 rows, and then work Row 1 one more time.

Front Right Leg

Setup: K18 sts, place remaining 18 sts on a piece of scrap yarn. Arrange sts on 3 dpns and join in the round. K2 (new EOR).

Knit 5 rounds.

Work joint.

Joint (all 4 worked the same)

Row 1: K5, turn work.
Row 2: Slip 1, P9, turn work.
Row 3: Slip 1, K9, turn work.
Row 4: Slip 1, P9.

Arrange sts on 2 dpns, hold side by side with RS together and work a 3-needle bind-off. Turn work RS out.

Stitches are now picked up along the top edge of work and joined with the live sts to work the bottom part of the leg.

Begin picking up sts at seam of 3-needle bind-off:

1st dpn: PU 5 sts along top left edge of work.
2nd dpn: K8 live sts.
3rd dpn: PU 5 sts along top right edge of work (EOR). (18 sts)

Join sts in the round to work the bottom of the leg.

Rnd 1: K all sts.
Rnd 2: K2tog, K14, SSK. (16 sts)
Rnds 3–4: K all sts.
Rnd 5: K2tog, K12, SSK. (14 sts)
Rnds 6–7: K all sts.
Rnd 8: K2tog, K10, SSK. (12 sts)

Rnds 9–12: K all sts.
Rnd 13: K2tog, K8, SSK. (10 sts)
Rnds 14–19: K all sts.
Rnd 20: K3, (M1, K1) 5 times, K2. (15 sts)
Rnd 21: K all sts.

Note: Rnd 22 contains several short rows within it. Work exactly as written.

Rnd 22: K11, w&t, P7, w&t, K8, w&t, P9, w&t, K12.

Cut yarn, thread through live sts, and pull closed. Seam hole at bottom of paw closed with the loose end.

Front Left Leg

Place 18 sts from scrap yarn onto 3 dpns. Rejoin yarn at first st, K18, join sts in the round. K16 (new EOR).

Repeat setup and all rounds, including the joint, the same as for the right leg.

Body

Seam together top 3 rows of chest, forming a circular opening that will be used for the neck and head.

Sts are now picked up along the back edges of the chest and down to the bottom of the joints and joined in the round to begin the body. Begin picking up sts at the top of the opening and pick up the following with 3 dpns:

1st dpn: PU 16 sts along the edge from top of opening down to top of leg, followed by 4 more sts from top of leg down to bottom of right leg joint.
2nd dpn: PU 4 sts from bottom of joint to center between legs, followed by 4 more sts to bottom of front left leg joint.
3rd dpn: PU 4 sts from bottom of joint to top of front left leg, followed by 16 more along the edge of work up to the top.

Sts can be rearranged on the needles after working a few rounds to more evenly distribute them. (48 sts)

Rnds 1–32: K all sts.

Rows 33–39 are short rows to shape the rear of the body.

Row 33: K6, w&t, P12, w&t, K6.
Row 34: K7, w&t, P14, w&t, K7.
Row 35: K8, w&t, P16, w&t, K5, place last 3 sts in row on a piece of scrap yarn together with the first 3 sts of the next round. CO 3 new sts to EOR.
Row 36: CO 3 new sts to working needle, K6, w&t, P18, w&t, K9.
Row 37: K10, w&t, P20, w&t, K10.
Row 38: K11, w&t, P22, w&t, K11.
Row 39: K12, w&t, K24, w&t, K12.

Back Right Leg

Rows 1–3 are short rows to curve the top of the leg.

Row 1: CO 2 new sts to working needle, K5, SSK, K2tog, K10, w&t, P19.
Row 2: K6, SSK, K2tog, K10, w&t, P18. (46 sts)
Row 3: K5, SSK, K2tog, K10, w&t, P17. (44 sts)

Setup for bottom of leg: K20, arrange these sts on 3 dpns; place remaining 24 sts on a piece of scrap yarn. Join first 20 sts in the round, K6 (new EOR).

K 4 rnds.

Work joint.

Sts are now picked up around the top edges of the joint to work the bottom of the leg. Begin picking up sts at seam of 3-needle bind-off:

1st dpn: PU 5 sts along top left edge of work.
2nd dpn: K2tog, K6, SSK.
3rd dpn: PU 5 sts along top right edge of work (EOR). (18 sts)

Join sts in the round.

Rnd 1: K all sts.
Rnd 2: K2tog, K14, SSK. (16 sts)
Rnd 3: K all sts.
Rnd 4: K2tog, K12, SSK. (14 sts)
Rnd 5: K all sts.
Rnd 6: K2tog, K10, SSK. (12 sts)
Rnd 7: K all sts.
Rnd 8: K2tog, K8, SSK. (10 sts)
Rnds 9–16: K all sts.
Rnd 17: K3, (M1, K1) 5 times, K2. (15 sts)
Rnd 18: K all sts.

Note: Rnd 19 contains several short rows within it. Work exactly as written.

Rnd 19: K11, w&t, P7, w&t, K8, w&t, P9, w&t, K12.

Cut yarn, thread through live sts, and pull closed. Seam hole at bottom of paw closed.

Back Left Leg

Rows 1–3 are short rows to curve the top of the leg.

CO 2 new sts to working needle and rejoin working yarn with purl side facing at first st on top (next to hole for tail).

Row 1: P5, P2tog, P2togtbl, P10, w&t, K19.
Row 2: P6, P2tog, P2togtbl, P10, w&t, K18. (22 sts)
Row 3: P5, P2tog, P2togtbl, P10, w&t, K17. (20 sts)

Arrange sts on 3 dpns and join in the round. K14 (new EOR).

Repeat setup and all rounds, including the joint, the same as for the right leg.

Tail Stump

Place the 6 live sts from scrap yarn onto 1 dpn. Sts are now picked up around the edge of the opening beneath the live sts to work the tail stump. Beginning in the bottom/center of the opening, PU the following number of sts on 3 dpns:

1st dpn: PU 5 sts from bottom/center to live sts on second dpn.
2nd dpn: K6.
3rd dpn: PU 5 sts from live sts to bottom/center (EOR). (16 sts)

Join sts in the round.

Rnds 1–2: K all sts.
Rnd 3: K2tog, K12, SSK. (14 sts)
Rnd 4: K all sts.

K3 with third dpn. Arrange sts evenly on 2 dpns; close with the Kitchener stitch.

Head

Sts are now picked up in the original CO sts to begin the head. Beginning at the center/back of opening, PU 36 sts with 3 dpns—1 st in each of the CO sts. Join sts in the round.

Rnds 1–2: K all sts.
Rnd 3: (M1, K2) 18 times. (54 sts)
Rnds 4–7: K all sts.
Rnd 8: K2, (SSK) 4 times, K34, (K2tog) 4 times, K2. (46 sts)
Rnd 9: K all sts.
Rnd 10: K3, (SSK) 4 times, K24, (K2tog) 4 times, K3. (38 sts)
Rnd 11: K all sts.
Rnd 12: K4, (SSK) 4 times, K14, (K2tog) 4 times, K4. (30 sts)
Rnd 13: K all sts.
Rnd 14: K5, (SSK) 4 times, K4, (K2tog) 4 times, K5. (22 sts)
Rnd 15: K all sts.

Rnd 16: K6, (SSK) 2 times, K2, (K2tog) 2 times, K6. (18 sts)
Rnd 17: K all sts.
Rnd 18: (K1, SSK) 3 times, (K2tog K1) 3 times. (12 sts)

Cut yarn, thread through remaining live sts, and pull closed.

Ears (make 2 the same)

The ears are worked separately and seamed to the top of the head. CO 12 sts onto 3 dpns and join in the round.

Rnds 1–3: K all sts.
Rnd 4: (K1, SSK, K2tog, K1) 2 times. (8 sts)
Rnds 5–7: K all sts.

Cut yarn and thread through remaining live sts; pull closed. Seam to head with the CO tail.

Stuff through hole between legs and then seam sides of the hole together.

Among the most prominent design features in Victorian-era houses were sash windows. Instead of being hinged, as the windows in older homes were, sash windows opened by sliding one pane over another. They improved ventilation and offered more natural light than the older windows, and their sills are the perfect thing for a cat to sit on.

Stand outside the Morgan family home on any day, and you are guaranteed to spy this particular cat in one of the home's many sash windows. Solitary and statuesque, he prefers to watch the world go by instead of chasing it in the garden.

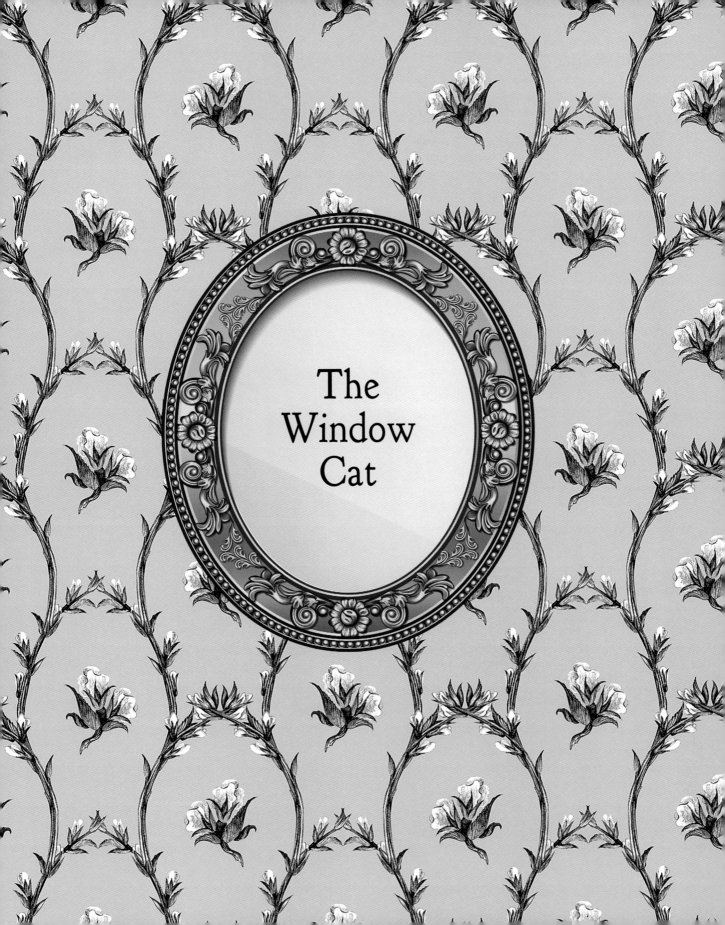

The
Window
Cat

FINISHED SIZE
- 13.5 in./34.5 cm tall
- 7.5 in./20 cm wide (not including tail)

YARN
Cascade Aereo: 180 yd./164.5 m total (striped cat: color A: 100 yd./91.5 m; color B: 80 yd./73 m)
- Black cat: 01 Jet
- Gray/white cat: 04 Ecru (A); 02 Charcoal (B)

NEEDLES
- US size 5/3.75 mm double-pointed needles

INSTRUCTIONS

Body

Note: For striped cat, CO color A, and knit 2 rnds of color A; after that, alternate colors every 3 rounds.

Work begins at side/bottom of body. CO 78 sts onto 3 or 4 dpns or a circular needle; join in the round.

Rnds 1–50: K all sts.
Rnd 51: (K2tog, K1) 2 times, K2tog, K62, (SSK, K1) 2 times, SSK. (72 sts)

Rnds 52–53: K all sts.
Rnd 54: (K2tog, K1) 2 times, K2tog, K56, (SSK, K1) 2 times, SSK. (66 sts)
Rnds 55–56: K all sts.
Rnd 57: (K2tog, K1) 2 times, K2tog, K50, (SSK, K1) 2 times, SSK. (60 sts)
Rnds 58–59: K all sts.
Rnd 60: (K2tog, K1) 2 times, K2tog, K44, (SSK, K1) 2 times, SSK. (54 sts)
Rnds 61–62: K all sts.
Rnd 63: (K2tog, K1) 2 times, K2tog, K38, (SSK, K1) 2 times, SSK. (48 sts)
Rnds 64–65: K all sts.
Rnd 66: (K2tog, K20, SSK) 2 times. (44 sts)
Rnds 67–68: K all sts.
Rnd 69: (K2tog, K18, SSK) 2 times. (40 sts)
Rnds 70–71: K all sts.

Head

Continuing with live sts.

Rnd 1: (K1, M1, K18, M1, K1) 2 times. (44 sts)
Rnds 2–3: K all sts.
Rnd 4: (K1, M1, K20, M1, K1) 2 times. (48 sts)
Rnds 5–6: K all sts.
Rnd 7: (K1, M1, K22, M1, K1) 2 times. (52 sts)
Rnds 8–9: K all sts.
Rnd 10: (K1, M1, K24, M1, K1) 2 times. (56 sts)
Rnds 11–12: K all sts.
Rnd 13: (K1, K2tog, K22, SSK, K1) 2 times. (52 sts)
Rnds 14–15: K all sts.
Rnd 16: (K1, K2tog, K20, SSK, K1) 2 times. (48 sts)
Rnds 17–18: K all sts.
Rnd 19: (K1, K2tog, K18, SSK, K1) 2 times. (44 sts)
Rnds 20–21: K all sts.

Ears

Slip the first 7 sts onto your working needle without knitting them. Slip next 30 sts onto a piece of scrap yarn. 14 sts remain on 2 needles. Arrange these on 3 dpns as follows: sts 1–5 on first dpn; sts 6–9 on second dpn; sts 10–14 on third dpn.

Rnds 1–3: K all sts. (14 sts)
Rnd 4: (SSK, K3, K2tog) 2 times. (10 sts)
Rnds 5–6: K all sts.
Rnd 7: (SSK, K1, K2tog) 2 times. (6 sts)
Rnd 8: K all sts.

Cut yarn, thread through remaining live sts, and pull closed.

Place the next 8 sts from scrap yarn onto a dpn. Place the last 8 sts from scrap yarn at the back of the head onto a second dpn. Close with the Kitchener stitch.

Arrange the 14 live sts onto 3 dpns as follows: sts 1–5 on first dpn; sts 6–9 on second dpn; sts 10–14 on third dpn. Repeat Rnds 1–8 of the other ear. Cut yarn, thread through remaining live sts, and pull closed.

Use loose ends to seam small hole on the inside of each ear closed. Stuff the ears, head, and top half of body now.

Base

PU 78 sts with 3 dpns in the original CO sts.

Rnd 1: K all sts.
Rnd 2: (K2tog, K4) 13 times. (65 sts)
Rnd 3: K all sts.
Rnd 4: (K2tog, K3) 13 times. (52 sts)
Rnd 5: K all sts.
Rnd 6: (K2tog, K2) 13 times. (39 sts)
Rnd 7: K all sts.
Rnd 8: (K2tog, K1) 13 times. (26 sts)
Rnd 9: K all sts.

Stuff the remainder of your cat now. Use a dpn to shift stuffing into the ears and distribute it evenly. This pattern was designed to be more of a silhouette than a three-dimensional object; keep this point in mind when stuffing—front to back should have a width of only about 3 in./7.5 cm.

Rnd 10: (K2tog) 13 times. (13 sts)
Rnd 11: K all sts.

Cut yarn, thread through remaining live sts, and pull closed. Weave in loose end.

Tail

CO 15 sts onto 3 dpns.

Knit all sts for 89 rounds or 12 in./30.5 cm.

Rnd 90: (K2tog, K3) 3 times. (12 sts)
Rnd 91: K all sts.

Cut yarn, thread through remaining live sts, and pull closed. Stuff all but 1 in./2.5 cm at open end. Sew this end fully opened to bottom of cat on the side with the decreases.

Paws (make 2 the same)

CO 15 sts onto 3 dpns and knit all sts for 14 rounds. Cut yarn, thread through live sts, and pull closed. Stuff half of paw and seam unstuffed half at the front of the body, opposite the tail.

Upper-class homeowners of the nineteenth century were expected to uphold a certain level of culture, and having a library was a good way to do this. A library would have reflected well on the owner, who benefited from the books even if he hadn't read them.

The entire Morgan family are keen readers, and the room is hardly ever empty. Timmy especially can be found here, lost in books about traveling and adventure on the high seas.

There is also a cat who likes to spend time in the library, benefiting from the room in a different way. While Timmy relishes the thrilling tales and mysteries of the Pacific Ocean, this cat relishes the warmth of the sunlight on the plush wool rug. While Mrs. Morgan researches where on the stem to prune a rose, this cat researches which chair has the most room to roll onto his back and relax spread-eagle without hitting anything.

The Library
Cat

FINISHED SIZE
- 17 in./43 cm long (not including tail)
- 8 in./20.5 cm wide

YARN
Woolfolk Tage Yarn: 260 yd./237.5 m total (color A/back: 180 yd./164.5 m; color B/belly: 80 yd./73 m)
- Cat 1: Color 24 (A: gray); Color 00 (B: white)
- Cat 2: Color 22 (A: dark taupe); Color 21 (B: light taupe)
- Cat 3: Back (A): Color 21 (light taupe) for 4 rows alternated with 2 rows of color 22 (dark taupe); Belly (B): Color 00 (white)

Note: Although this yarn is classified as worsted weight on Ravelry, it is more like a fingering or light DK weight when knitted for a stuffed animal. If looking for a substitute yarn to use on this project, please keep that point in mind.

NEEDLES
- US size 3/3.25 mm straight needles
- US size 3/3.25 mm double-pointed needles

NOTES
- "Right" and "left" refer to the cat's right and left throughout the pattern.
- All increases are notated as "CO 1." This refers to the backwards loop method of casting on a stitch to the working needle. If using the recommended yarn or another yarn that is "hairy," this is the best increase to use. However, if using a plain, non-hairy or non-furry yarn, this increase may leave a hole, so any other increase can be substituted.
- For clarification while knitting, the back legs are referred to as legs, and the front legs are referred to as arms.

INSTRUCTIONS

Back (bottom of cat)

The back is worked flat; turn work after each row. Work begins at neckline. CO 20 color A sts onto 1 straight needle.

Row 1 (WS): P all sts.
Row 2 (RS): K1, CO 1, K18, CO 1, K1. (22 sts)
Row 3: P all sts.
Row 4: K1, CO 1, K20, CO 1, K1. (24 sts)
Row 5: P all sts.
Row 6: K1, CO 1, K22, CO 1, K1. (26 sts)
Row 7: P all sts.
Row 8: K1, CO 1, K24, CO 1, K1. (28 sts)
Row 9: P all sts.
Row 10: K1, CO 1, K26, CO 1, K1. (30 sts)
Row 11: P all sts.
Row 12: K1, CO 1, K28, CO 1, K1. (32 sts)
Row 13: P all sts.
Row 14: K all sts.
Row 15: P all sts; place removable st marker on first and last st of this row.

Row 16: K1, CO 1, K30, CO 1, K1. (34 sts)
Row 17: P all sts.
Row 18: K all sts.
Row 19: P all sts.
Row 20: K1, CO 1, K32, CO 1, K1. (36 sts)
Row 21: P all sts.
Row 22: K all sts.
Row 23: P all sts.
Row 24: K1, CO 1, K34, CO 1, K1. (38 sts)
Row 25: P all sts.
Row 26: K all sts; place removable st marker on first and last st of this row.
Row 27: P all sts.
Row 28: K1, CO 1, K36, CO 1, K1. (40 sts)
Row 29: P all sts.
Row 30: K all sts.
Row 31: P all sts.
Row 32: K1, CO 1, K38, CO 1, K1. (42 sts)
Row 33: P all sts.
Row 34: K all sts.
Row 35: P all sts.
Row 36: K41, CO 1, K1. (43 sts)
Row 37: P all sts.
Row 38: K all sts.
Row 39: P all sts.
Row 40: K42, CO 1, K1. (44 sts)
Row 41: P all sts.

Row 42: K all sts.
Row 43: P all sts.
Row 44: K43, CO 1, K1. (45 sts)
Row 45: P all sts.
Row 46: K all sts.
Row 47: P all sts.
Row 48: K44, CO 1, K1. (46 sts)
Row 49: P all sts.
Row 50: K all sts.
Row 51: P all sts.
Row 52: K45, CO 1, K1. (47 sts)
Row 53: P all sts.
Row 54: K all sts.
Row 55: P all sts.
Row 56: K1, CO 1, K46. (48 sts)
Row 57: P all sts.
Row 58: K all sts.
Row 59: P all sts.
Row 60: K1, CO 1, K47. (49 sts)
Row 61: P all sts.
Row 62: K all sts.
Row 63: P all sts.
Row 64: K all sts.
Row 65: P all sts.
Row 66: K1, CO 1, K48. (50 sts)
Row 67: P all sts.
Row 68: K all sts.
Row 69: P all sts.
Row 70: K21, place 8 sts on scrap yarn, CO 8 new sts to working needle, K21.
Row 71: P all sts.
Row 72: K1, CO 1, K49. (51 sts)
Row 73: P all sts.
Row 74: K all sts.
Row 75: P all sts.
Row 76: K all sts.
Row 77: P all sts.
Row 78: K1, CO 1, K50. (52 sts)
Row 79: P all sts.

Back Side Right Leg

Setup: K26, place 26 on scrap yarn. (26 sts)

Row 1: P all sts.
Row 2: K all sts.
Row 3: P all sts.
Row 4: SSK, K22, K2tog. (24 sts)
Row 5: P all sts.
Row 6: K all sts.
Row 7: P all sts.
Row 8: SSK, K20, K2tog. (22 sts)
Row 9: P all sts.
Row 10: K all sts.
Row 11: P all sts.
Row 12: SSK, K18, K2tog. (20 sts)
Row 13: P all sts.
Row 14: (SSK) 2 times, K12, (K2tog) 2 times. (16 sts)
Row 15: P all sts.
Row 16: (SSK) 2 times, K8, (K2tog) 2 times. (12 sts)
Row 17: P all sts.
Row 18: (SSK) 2 times, K4, (K2tog) 2 times. (8 sts)

Cut yarn, place live sts on scrap yarn or 1 dpn.

Back Side Left Leg

Place 26 live sts from scrap yarn onto 1 dpn or straight needle. With RS facing, rejoin color A at first st; K26. Repeat Rows 1–18 the same as the other leg.

Belly (top)

The belly is worked flat; turn work after each row. CO 16 color B sts onto 1 dpn or straight needle.

Row 1 (WS): P all sts.
Row 2 (RS): K1, CO 1, K14, CO 1, K1. (18 sts)
Row 3: P all sts.
Row 4: K1, CO 1, K16, CO 1, K1. (20 sts)
Row 5: P all sts.
Row 6: K1, CO 1, K18, CO 1, K1. (22 sts)
Rows 7–35: Work 29 rows of stockinette stitch, knitting all sts on the RS and purling all sts on the WS. Place a removable stitch marker on the first and last sts of Rows 15 and 26.
Row 36: K1, CO 1, K21. (23 sts)
Row 37: P all sts.
Row 38: K all sts.
Row 39: P all sts.
Row 40: K1, CO 1, K22. (24 sts)
Row 41: P all sts.
Row 42: K all sts.
Row 43: P all sts.
Row 44: K1, CO 1, K23. (25 sts)
Row 45: P all sts.
Row 46: K all sts.
Row 47: P all sts.
Row 48: K1, CO 1, K24. (26 sts)
Row 49: P all sts.
Row 50: K all sts.
Row 51: P all sts.
Row 52: K1, CO 1, K25. (27 sts)
Row 53: P all sts.
Row 54: K all sts.
Row 55: P all sts.
Row 56: K26, CO 1, K1. (28 sts)
Row 57: P all sts.
Row 58: K all sts.
Row 59: P all sts.
Row 60: K27, CO 1, K1. (29 sts)
Row 61: P all sts.
Row 62: K all sts.
Row 63: P all sts.
Row 64: K all sts.
Row 65: P all sts.
Row 66: K28, CO 1, K1. (30 sts)

Row 67: P all sts.
Row 68: K all sts.
Row 69: P all sts.
Row 70: K all sts.
Row 71: P all sts.
Row 72: K29, CO 1, K1. (31 sts)
Row 73: P all sts.
Row 74: K all sts.
Row 75: P all sts.
Row 76: K all sts.
Row 77: P all sts.
Row 78: K30, CO 1, K1. (32 sts)
Row 79: P all sts.

Belly Side Right Leg

Setup: K16, place 16 sts on scrap yarn. (16 sts)

Row 1: P all sts.
Row 2: K all sts.
Row 3: P all sts.
Row 4: SSK, K12, K2tog. (14 sts)
Row 5: P all sts.
Row 6: K all sts.
Row 7: P all sts.
Row 8: SSK, K10, K2tog. (12 sts)
Row 9: P all sts.
Row 10: K all sts.
Row 11: P all sts.
Row 12: SSK, K8, K2tog. (10 sts)

Row 13: P all sts.
Row 14: SSK, K6, K2tog. (8 sts)
Row 15: P all sts.
Row 16: SSK, K4, K2tog. (6 sts)
Row 17: P all sts.
Row 18: K all sts.

Cut yarn, leave sts on scrap yarn or 1 dpn.

Belly Side Left Leg

Place 16 live sts from scrap yarn onto 1 dpn. With RS facing, rejoin color B at first st; K16. Repeat Rows 1–18 the same as the other leg.

After both legs are worked, back and belly pieces are held with WS facing each other to work the feet.

Right Foot

Setup: Arrange the 8 color A live sts onto 2 dpns. These sts are joined in the round with the live color B sts on a third dpn. With RS facing, rejoin color B yarn at 1st color A st, K8, and then K6 color B sts (EOR). (14 sts)

Rnds 1–2: K all sts.

The following short rows will shape the heel and are worked on both sides of the EOR; knitting in the round is resumed in Rnd 10.

Row 3: K4, w&t.
Row 4: P3, w&t.
Row 5: K4, w&t.
Row 6: P5, w&t.
Row 7: K6, w&t.
Row 8: P7, w&t.
Row 9: K1 (EOR).
Rnd 10: K all sts.
Rnd 11: K1, SSK, K2tog, K9. (12 sts)
Rnds 12–26: K all sts.
Rnd 27: K7, CO 1, K2, CO 1, K3. (14 sts)
Rnds 28–29: K all sts.

Cut yarn, thread through remaining live sts, and pull closed.

Left Foot

Arrange the 8 live color A sts onto 2 dpns. These sts are joined in the round with the live color B sts on a third dpn. With RS facing, rejoin color B yarn at first color A st, K8 (EOR). **Note:** The EOR is in a different place than it was on the right foot. (14 sts)

Rnds 1–2: K all sts.

The following short rows will shape the heel and are worked on both sides of the EOR; knitting in the round is resumed in Rnd 10.

Row 3: K13, w&t.
Row 4: P3, w&t.
Row 5: K4, w&t.
Row 6: P5, w&t.
Row 7: K6, w&t.
Row 8: P7, w&t.
Row 9: K6 (EOR).
Rnd 10: K all sts.
Rnd 11: K9, SSK, K2tog, K1. (12 sts)
Rnds 12–26: K all sts.
Rnd 27: K5, CO 1, K2, CO 1, K5. (14 sts)
Rnds 28–29: K all sts.

Cut yarn, thread through remaining live sts, and pull closed.

Seaming Belly and Back Together

With WS together, begin from outside of heel on either leg and, with color B, whipstitch the edges of the 2 pieces together up to the lower stitch marker; then cut yarn, secure, and begin again from the upper stitch marker to the original CO sts. Repeat on the other side.

Leave the inner leg seams open until the ears have been knit and it's time to stuff your cat. **Note:** The original CO sts can be a little difficult to differentiate from the "shoulder" sts. Make sure to seam all the way up to them so that the opening left for the neck is only 20 color A and 16 color B sts.

Tail

Setup: Place 8 color A sts from scrap yarn on the back piece onto 2 dpns. With RS facing, rejoin color A at 5th st, K4. With 2 additional dpns, PU 10 sts around edges of opening, K4 (EOR). (18 sts)

Rnd 1: K all sts.

Short rows are now worked on both sides of the EOR to change the direction of the sts, pointing them downward. Knitting in the round is resumed in Rnd 7.

Row 2: K4, w&t.
Row 3: P8, w&t.
Row 4: K9, w&t.
Row 5: P10, w&t.

Row 6: K5 (EOR).
Rnds 7–16: K all sts.
Rnd 17: K2tog, K14, SSK. (16 sts)
Rnds 18–77: K all sts (60 rnds or about 7 additional inches/18 cm).
Rnd 78: K2tog, K12, SSK. (14 sts)
Rnd 79: K all sts.
Rnd 80: K2tog, K10, SSK. (12 sts)

Cut yarn, thread through remaining live sts, and pull closed.

Arms (work both the same)

Setup: With RS facing, begin at bottom/center of opening and PU 24 sts around the edges; use color A and 3 dpns.

Rnd 1: K all sts.

Short rows are worked to change the direction of the sts. Knitting in the round is resumed in Rnd 5.

Row 2: K22, w&t.
Row 3: P20, w&t.
Row 4: K22 (EOR).
Rnds 5–6: K all sts.
Rnd 7: K2tog, K20, SSK. (22 sts)
Rnds 8–9: K all sts.
Rnd 10: K2tog, K18, SSK. (20 sts)
Rnds 11–12: K all sts.
Rnd 13: K2tog, K16, SSK. (18 sts)

Rnds 14–15: K all sts.
Rnd 16: K2tog, K14, SSK. (16 sts)
Rnds 17–18: K all sts.
Rnd 19: K2tog, K12, SSK. (14 sts)
Rnds 20–21: K all sts.
Rnd 22: K2tog, K10, SSK. (12 sts)

The following short rows will bend the wrist. Knitting in the round is resumed in Rnd 30.

Row 23: K11, w&t.
Row 24: P10, w&t.
Row 25: K8, w&t.
Row 26: P6, w&t.
Row 27: K4, w&t.
Row 28: P2, w&t.
Row 29: K7 (EOR).
Rnd 30: K all sts.
Rnd 31: (K4, CO 1) 2 times, K4. (14 sts)
Rnds 32–35: K all sts.

Cut yarn, thread through live sts, and pull closed.

Head

Sts are now picked up in the original CO sts to begin the head. It is worked flat and in 2 parts—the back with color A and the front with color B. The parts will fit together like puzzle pieces when completed.

Front of Head

Setup: With RS facing and color B yarn, begin on the far right side of the color B CO sts and PU 18 sts across the front (belly) of your cat. **Note:** This is 2 more sts than the CO number of 16.

Row 1 (WS): P all sts.
Row 2 (RS): K all sts.
Row 3: P all sts.
Row 4: K all sts.
Row 5: P all sts.
Row 6: SSK, K14, K2tog. (16 sts)
Row 7: P all sts.
Row 8: SSK, K12, K2tog. (14 sts)
Row 9: P all sts.

Work Rows 10 and 12 exactly as written; there are multiple short rows within each.

K15, place a st marker or divide sts onto 2 dpns. Rows 1–9 are short rows that will each begin and end at the st marker and are worked back and forth on both sides of it.

Row 1: K6, w&t, P12, w&t, K6.
Row 2: K8, w&t, P16, w&t, K8.
Row 3: K10, w&t, P20, w&t, K10.
Row 4: K12, w&t, P24, w&t, K12.
Row 5: K14, w&t, P28, w&t, K14.
Row 6: K12, w&t, P24, w&t, K12.
Row 7: K10, w&t, P20, w&t, K10.
Row 8: K8, w&t, P16, w&t, K8.
Row 9: K6, w&t, P12, w&t, K6.
Row 10: K15 (EOR).

The sts will now be divided into 2 sections. Each section, when finished, is folded down to fit on the outsides of the color B (front of head) section and seamed together. The 2 sections are both worked with color A yarn.

Left Side of Head

Row 1: Bind off 10 sts purlwise, P4, place next 15 on scrap yarn. (5 sts)
Row 2: SSK, (CO 1, K1) 3 times. (7 sts)
Row 3: P all sts.
Row 4: SSK, K2, (CO, K1) 3 times. (9 sts)
Row 5: P all sts.
Row 6: SSK, K4, (CO 1, K1) 3 times. (11 sts)
Row 7: P all sts.
Row 8: SSK, K9. (10 sts)
Row 9: P all sts.
Row 10: SSK, K6, K2tog. (8 sts)
Row 11: P all sts.
Row 12: SSK, K6. (7 sts)
Row 13: P all sts.
Row 14: SSK, K3, K2tog. (5 sts)
Row 15: P all sts.
Row 16: SSK, K3. (4 sts)
Row 17: P all sts.
Row 18: SSK, K2tog. (2 sts)
Row 19: P all sts.
Row 20: SSK. (1 st)

Cut yarn, pull through last st.

Row 10: SSK, K9, w&t, P8, w&t, K9, K2tog. (12 sts)
Row 11: P all sts.
Row 12: SSK, K7, w&t, P6, w&t, K7, K2tog. (10 sts)
Row 13: P all sts.
Row 14: SSK, K6, K2tog. (8 sts)
Row 15: P all sts.
Row 16: SSK, K4, K2tog. (6 sts)
Row 17: P all sts.
Row 18: SSK, K2, K2tog. (4 sts)
Row 19: P all sts.
Row 20: SSK, K2tog. (2 sts)
Row 21: P all sts.
Row 22: K2tog. (1 st)

Cut yarn, thread through the last st, and pull closed.

Back of Head

The back of the head is worked in 3 parts—the back, the left side, and the right side.

Back setup: With RS facing and color A yarn, begin on the far right side of the color A CO sts. (PU2, CO 1) 10 times. (30 sts)

Row 1 (WS): P all sts.
Row 2 (RS): K all sts.

Repeat the last 2 rows 4 more times for a total of 10 rows worked in stockinette st, and then repeat Row 1 one more time.

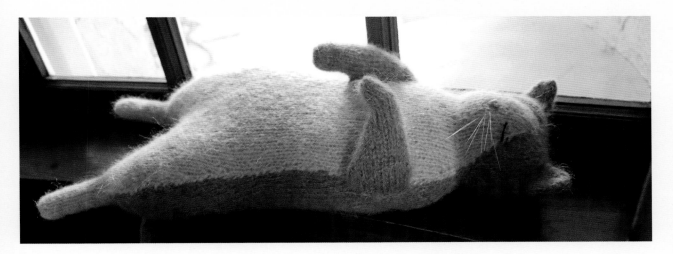

Right Side of Head

Place 15 sts from scrap yarn onto 1 dpn. With RS facing, rejoin color A at first st.

Row 1: Bind off 10 sts, K4. (5 sts)
Row 2: P all sts.
Row 3: (K1, CO 1) 3 times, K2tog. (7 sts)
Row 4: P all sts.
Row 5: (K1, CO 1) 3 times, K2, K2tog. (9 sts)
Row 6: P all sts.
Row 7: (K1, CO 1) 3 times, K4, K2tog. (11 sts)
Row 8: P all sts.
Row 9: K9, K2tog. (10 sts)
Row 10: P all sts.
Row 11: SSK, K6, K2tog. (8 sts)
Row 12: P all sts.
Row 13: K6, K2tog. (7 sts)
Row 14: P all sts.
Row 15: SSK, K3, K2tog. (5 sts)
Row 16: P all sts.
Row 17: K3, K2tog. (4 sts)
Row 18: P all sts.
Row 19: SSK, K2tog. (2 sts)
Row 20: P all sts.
Row 21: K2tog. (1 st)

Cut yarn, pull through last st. Hold back sides alongside the front piece and seam together on both sides. Then seam the outer edges of the 2 pieces to the back of the head, from the bottom up to what looks like a corner (where the bind-off sts began) on each side. The openings left at the top are for the ears.

Ears (work 2 the same)

Sts are now picked up in the openings at top of head to work the ears.

Setup: With RS facing, begin in the front/center of one of the openings and PU 16 sts with color A and 3 dpns. Join sts in the round.

Rnds 1–4: K all sts.
Rnd 5: K2, K2tog, SSK, K4, K2tog, SSK, K2. (12 sts)
Rnds 6–9: K all sts.
Rnd 10: K1, K2tog, SSK, K2, K2tog, SSK, K1. (8 sts)

Cut yarn, thread through remaining live sts, and pull closed.

Finishing

The cat is stuffed from the opening between the back legs. The head is stuffed fully; ears are left unstuffed and flattened. Arms, legs, and tail are stuffed moderately, and the body is stuffed lightly so that it appears more flat than round.

Seam the edges of the inner legs together.

Arms can be left outstretched as they naturally fall, or one or both of them can be tacked to the body into desired position.

Timothy Morgan is never still. Even when it's raining outside and he's prone with a book on the library rug, his lower legs are raised and swinging back and forth like the pendulum of a clock. He and Trudy are schooled at home, but Mrs. Morgan is beginning to wonder whether they wouldn't be better off at a private school.

"Master" Timmy (as young sons in Victorian families are addressed) is known for the pranks he pulls on everyone in the household, servants included. His favorite one is to put a frog in Cook's apron pocket when she's not looking. She threatens to make a soup out of it if he does it again but secretly enjoys his antics. When asked what he wants to be when he grows up, Timmy's answer hasn't changed since he was two years old: "I want to be the captain of a ship."

Timmy's cat is a young tuxedo who gets in as much trouble as he does. The goldfish in the parlour bowl have had to be replaced three times now by Mrs. Morgan (hard to pull off without Trudy knowing—good thing most goldfish look the same).

Master Timmy's Tuxedo

FINISHED SIZE

- 10 in./25.5 cm tall
- 4.5 in./11.5 cm wide
- 8 in./20.5 cm deep (not including tail)

YARN

Berroco Vintage Chunky: 170 yd./155.5 m total
(color A: 140 yd./128 m; color B: 30 yd./27.5 m)

- Cat 1: 6145 Cast Iron (A); 6100 Snow Day (B)
- Cat 2: 6107 Cracked Pepper (A);
  6100 Snow Day (B)
- Cat 3: 6176 Pumpkin (A); 6100 Snow Day (B)

NEEDLES

- US size 5/3.75 mm straight needles
- US size 5/3.75 mm double-pointed needles

INSTRUCTIONS

Chest

Work begins at neckline and is worked flat with
the intarsia method of colorwork. When switching
colors, always remember to bring the new color
over the old one to prevent a gap from forming
between them.

Begin by preparing a second ball of color A (about
20 armlengths), so that you'll have one ball for each
side of the needle with the color B sts in the center.
What is left over from this second ball of color A
can be used for the head, which is also worked with
intarsia. CO the following colors and numbers of sts
onto one straight needle:

- Color A: CO 8 sts (larger ball)
- Color B: CO 20 sts
- Color A: CO 8 sts (smaller ball) (36 sts)

Row 1: Color A: P8; Color B: P20; Color A: P8.
Row 2: Color A: K8; Color B: K20; Color A: K8.
Row 3: Color A: P8; Color B: P20; Color A: P8.
Row 4: Color A: K8; Color B: K20; Color A: K8.
Row 5: Color A: P8; Color B: P20; Color A: P8.
Row 6: Color A: K9; Color B: K18; Color A: K9.
Row 7: Color A: P9; Color B: P18; Color A: P9.
Row 8: Color A: K9; Color B: K18; Color A: K9.
Row 9: Color A: P9; Color B: P18; Color A: P9.

Row 10: Color A: K10; Color B: K16; Color
A: K10.
Row 11: Color A: P10; Color B: P16; Color A: P10.
Row 12: Color A: K10; Color B: K16; Color
A: K10.
Row 13: Color A: P10; Color B: P16; Color A: P10.
Row 14: Color A: K11; Color B: K14; Color
A: K11.
Row 15: Color A: P11; Color B: P14; Color A: P11.
Row 16: Color A: K11; Color B: K14; Color
A: K11.
Row 17: Color A: P11; Color B: P14; Color A: P11.
Row 18: Color A: K12; Color B: K12; Color
A: K12.
Row 19: Color A: P12; Color B: P12; Color A: P12.
Row 20: Color A: K12; Color B: K12; Color
A: K12.
Row 21: Color A: P12; Color B: P12; Color A: P12.
Row 22: Color A: K13; Color B: K10; Color
A: K13.

Row 23: Color A: P13; Color B: P10; Color A: P13.
Row 24: Color A: K13; Color B: K10; Color A: K13.
Row 25: Color A: P13; Color B: P10; Color A: P13.
Row 26: Color A: K14; Color B: K8; Color A: K14.
Row 27: Color A: P14; Color B: P8; Color A: P14.
Row 28: Color A: K14; Color B: K8; Color A: K14.
Row 29: Color A: P14; Color B: P8; Color A: P14.

Cut color B and small ball of color A.

Right Leg

Upper leg setup: K18 (all with the larger ball of color A), place remaining 18 sts on scrap yarn. Arrange the 18 just knit sts onto 3 dpns; join in the round. Rows 2–5 are short rows to shape the back of the "elbow." Turn work after each one.

Rnd 1: K all sts.
Row 2: K7, turn work.
Row 3: Slip 1, P7.
Row 4: Slip 1, K7.
Row 5: Slip 1, P7.

Arrange these 8 sts onto 2 dpns, 4 on each, and turn RS facing each other. Work a 3-needle bind-off. Cut yarn and pull through last st. Turn work RS out.

Lower leg setup: Rejoin color A at bind-off seam and PU or knit the following sts with 3 dpns:

1st dpn: PU 4 from bind-off seam along the edge up to live sts, K2.
2nd dpn: K6 of the live sts.
3rd dpn: K2, PU 4 along edge to bind-off seam (EOR). (18 sts)

Rnds 1–3: K all sts.
Rnd 4: K2tog, K14, SSK. (16 sts)
Rnds 5–9: K all sts.
Rnd 10: K2tog, K12, SSK. (14 sts)
Rnds 11–15: K all sts.
Rnd 16: K2tog, K10, SSK. (12 sts)
Rnds 17–21: K all sts.

Cut color A; join color B.

Rnds 22–24: K all sts.
Rnd 25: K5, (M1, K1) 3 times, K4. (15 sts)
Rnds 26–27: K all sts.
Rnd 28: K10, w&t, P5, w&t, K6, w&t, P7, w&t, K11.

Cut yarn, thread through live sts, and pull closed. Weave in loose end.

Left Leg

Upper leg setup: Place 18 sts from scrap yarn onto 1 dpn. With RS facing, rejoin color A at 1st st, K18. Arrange sts onto 3 dpns; join in the round. Rows 2–5 are short rows to shape the back of the "elbow." Turn work after each one.

Rnd 1: K all sts.
Row 2: K1, turn work.
Row 3: Slip 1, P7.
Row 4: Slip 1, K7.
Row 5: Slip 1, P7.

Work the rest of the elbow and lower leg instructions the same as for the right one.

Body

Setup: Hold first and last CO sts together and seam top 3 rows together, forming a circle that will serve as the neck opening. Beginning at the top/center of that circle (just below the seam), and with RS facing, rejoin color A and PU the following sts along the edge of the chest with 3 dpns:

1st dpn: PU 28 sts along the right edge from top/center down to the right elbow (about 1 st for every 1 row).
2nd dpn: PU 12 sts along the edge from the right elbow across to the left elbow.
3rd dpn: PU 28 sts along the left edge from left elbow up to the top/center (about 1 st for every 1 row). (68 sts)

Rnd 1: K all sts.
Rnd 2: (K2tog) 2 times, K60, (SSK) 2 times. (64 sts)
Rnd 3: K all sts.
Rnd 4: (K2tog) 2 times, K56, (SSK) 2 times. (60 sts)
Rnd 5: K all sts.
Rnd 6: (K2tog) 2 times, K52, (SSK) 2 times. (56 sts)
Rnd 7: K all sts.
Rnd 8: (K2tog) 2 times, K48, (SSK) 2 times. (52 sts)
Rnds 9–13: K all sts.

Short rows are now worked to change the direction of the sts and curve the back downward. Each of these rows below has 2 short rows within it—one on the knit side of the fabric and one on the purl side—and each one begins and ends at the EOR. Knitting in the round resumes in Rnd 31.

Row 14: K4, w&t, P8, w&t, K4.
Row 15: K5, w&t, P10, w&t, K5.
Row 16: K6, w&t, P12, w&t, K6.
Row 17: K7, w&t, P14, w&t, K7.
Row 18: K8, w&t, P16, w&t, K8.
Row 19: K9, w&t, P18, w&t, K9.
Row 20: K10, w&t, P20, w&t, K10.
Row 21: K11, w&t, P22, w&t, K11.
Row 22: K12, w&t, P24, w&t, K12.
Row 23: K13, w&t, P26, w&t, K13.
Row 24: K14, w&t, P28, w&t, K14.
Row 25: K15, w&t, P30, w&t, K15.
Row 26: K16, w&t, P32, w&t, K16.
Row 27: K17, w&t, P34, w&t, K17.
Row 28: K18, w&t, P36, w&t, K18.
Row 29: K19, w&t, P38, w&t, K19.
Row 30: K20, w&t, P40, w&t, K20.
Rnds 31–46: K all sts.

Cut yarn. Place all sts on a piece of scrap yarn while the head is being worked.

Head

Sts are now picked up in the original CO sts to work the head. Although it is worked flat, 3 dpns are used to hold the sts so they curve into a U-shape with the opening at the back. The head is worked with intarsia, and the second ball of color A that was prepared for the chest is used again.

Setup: With RS facing, begin at the first color A st at back of neck. Pick up the following number and color of sts:

1st dpn: Color A: PU 8 sts in the color A CO sts.
2nd dpn: Color B: PU 20 sts in the color B CO sts.
3rd dpn: Color A: PU 8 sts in the color A CO sts. (36 sts)

Row 1: Color A: P8 (8 sts); Color B: P20 (20 sts); Color A: P8 (8 sts).
Row 2: Color A: SSK, K2, (M1, K1) 4 times (11 sts); Color B: (M1, K2) 10 times (30 sts); Color A: (M1, K1) 4 times, K2, K2tog (11 sts).
Row 3: Color A: P11; Color B: P30 (carry color A behind for the first 8 sts); Color A: P11.
Row 4: Color A: SSK, K18 (carry color B behind sts 11–18) (19 sts); Color B: K12 (12 sts); Color A: K18, K2tog (19 sts).
Row 5: Color A: P19; Color B: P12; Color A: P19.
Row 6: Color A: SSK, K18 (19 sts); Color B: K10 (10 sts); Color A: K18, K2tog (19 sts).
Row 7: Color A: P19; Color B: P10; Color A: P19.

The color B section of the following row contains several short rows within it that will create the cat's snout. Work these exactly as written.

Row 8: Color A: SSK, K17 (18 sts); Color B: K9, w&t, P8, w&t, K7, w&t, P6, w&t, K5, w&t, P4, w&t, K7; Color A: K17, K2tog (18 sts).
Row 9: Color A: P18; Color B: P10; Color A: P18.
Row 10: Color A: SSK, K12, SSK, K2tog, K1 (16 sts); Color B: K8 (8 sts); Color A: K1, SSK, K2tog, K12, K2tog (16 sts).
Row 11: Color A: P16; Color B: P8; Color A: P16.
Row 12: Color A: SSK, K10, SSK, K2tog, K1 (14 sts); Color B: K6 (6 sts); Color A: K1, SSK, K2tog, K10, K2tog (14 sts).
Row 13: Color A: P14; Color B: P6; Color A: P14.
Row 14: Color A: SSK, K8, SSK, K2tog, K1 (12 sts); Color B: K4 (4 sts); Color A: K1, SSK, K2tog, K8, K2tog (12 sts).
Row 15: Color A: P14; Color B: P4; Color A: P14.
Row 16: Color A: SSK, K6, SSK, K2tog, K1 (10 sts); Color B: K2 (2 sts); Color A: K1, SSK, K2tog, K6, K2tog (10 sts).
Row 17: Color A: P10; Color B: P2; Color A: P10.

Cut color B and the second ball of color A. The remainder is worked with one ball of color A only.

Row 18: SSK, K4, SSK, K2tog, K2, SSK, K2tog, K4, K2tog. (16 sts)
Row 19: P all sts.
Row 20: SSK, K2, (SSK, K2tog) 2 times, K2, K2tog. (10 sts)

Cut yarn leaving a tail for seaming back of head, thread through remaining live sts, and pull closed. Seam back of head closed.

Stuff head, chest area, and front legs all fully now before working the base. Use a dpn from the outside to help move the stuffing down into the paws, which are bent slightly forward. Stuff legs and thighs so that they are straight and stiff enough to support the body when finished. Do not stuff the back of the body yet.

Note: The top of the head will need to be flattened after stuffing. The head was designed to have extra fabric at the top, so that, when stuffed and flattened, it will make the face fuller on the sides. Not flattening the top of the head will give it a narrow, cone-shaped appearance.

Base

Place 52 sts from scrap yarn back onto dpns. Rejoin color A at first st.

Rnd 1: K49, place last 3 sts in rnd plus first 3 sts from next rnd onto a piece of scrap yarn, CO 3 new sts to EOR.
Rnd 2: CO 3 new sts to working needle, K49.
Rnd 3: K all sts.
Rnd 4: (K2, K2tog) 13 times. (39 sts)
Rnd 5: K all sts.
Rnd 6: (K1, K2tog) 13 times. (26 sts)
Rnd 7: K all sts.

Finish stuffing the rest of the body fully now. Use a dpn from the outside to shift additional stuffing up into the chest, upper legs, and upper body as you add more to the bottom. This young cat takes more stuffing than you would think.

Rnd 8: (K2tog) 13 times. (13 sts)
Rnds 9–10: K all sts.

Cut yarn, thread through remaining live sts, and pull closed. Weave in loose end. Base is flattened to provide firm seating.

Tail

Setup: Place 6 live sts from scrap yarn onto a dpn. With RS facing, begin at the bottom/center of the opening beneath the live sts and begin picking up the following sts (18 sts):

1st dpn: PU 6 sts along the left edge from bottom/center of opening up to live sts.
2nd dpn: K6 live sts.
3rd dpn: PU 6 sts along the right edge from live sts down to bottom/center of opening.

Note: The tail will need to be stuffed (loosely) a little at a time as you proceed.

Rnds 1–5: K all sts.
Rnd 6: K2tog, K14, SSK. (16 sts)
Rnds 7–11: K all sts.
Rnd 12: K2tog, K12, SSK. (14 sts)
Rnds 13–17: K all sts.
Rnd 18: K2tog, K10, SSK. (12 sts)
Rnds 19–42: K all sts.
Rnd 43: K2tog, K8, SSK. (10 sts)
Rnds 44–45: K all sts.
Rnd 46: K2tog, K6, SSK. (8 sts)
Rnds 47–48: K all sts.

Cut yarn, thread through remaining live sts, and pull closed. Weave in loose end.

Ears (make 2 the same)

CO 12 color A sts onto 3 dpns; join in the round.

Rnds 1–3: K all sts.
Rnd 4: (K1, SSK, K2tog, K1) 2 times. (8 sts)
Rnds 5–7: K all sts.

Cut yarn, thread through remaining live sts, and pull closed. Use the loose end to enhance point at top. Flatten with EOR in the front/center; stretch and shape into triangle. Seam to head with CO tail.

Back Feet (work both the same)

CO 12 color B sts onto 3 dpns; join in the round.

Rnds 1–10: K all sts.
Rnd 11: K5, (M1, K1) 3 times, K4. (15 sts)
Rnds 12–13: K all sts.
Rnd 14: K10, w&t, P5, w&t, K6, w&t, P7, w&t, K11.

Cut yarn, thread through live sts, and pull closed. Stuff very lightly from the CO end, which is left open. Seam about one-third of each foot to the base, with increases on the top side. Feet should be 0.25–0.5 in./0.5–1.25 cm apart from each other.

The potting shed is an ideal place for a mother cat to bear and raise a litter of kittens. Dark corners with low shelving provide protection and almost completely hide this anxious mother, who made her way into the shed through a broken window after making the acquaintance of the garden cat.

The only person for a long time (since the gardener left) to come into the shed has been Mrs. Morgan—this is where she starts her tomato seedlings and where she keeps the pruning shears. One day, while repotting some young plants, she saw something moving in the corner and, realizing what it was, she turned around immediately and walked out. After all, Mrs. Morgan is familiar with the pressures of raising multiples.

The Potting Shed
Cat and Kittens

FINISHED SIZE
- **Mother Cat:** 20 in./51 cm long (not including tail); 6 in./15 cm wide (not including legs)
- **Kitten:** 4.5 in./11.5 cm long (not including tail); 1.5 in./4 cm wide (not including legs)

YARN
Cascade Aereo: Cat: 280 yd./256 m; Kitten: 20 yd./18.5 m
- Dark gray cat: 02 Charcoal
- Light gray cat: 03 Silver
- White cat: 04 Ecru

Note: You will also need an additional 1–2 yd./1–2 m of pink worsted weight yarn for the nipples.

NEEDLES
- US size 5/3.75 mm double-pointed needles

NOTE
Picking up and knitting the wraps after the short rows in this pattern is optional. You may decide to pick them up in some places but not in others. Personally, I picked up the wraps and knit them along with the stitch on the knit side of the body only but found that leaving them alone looked best on the purl side and in other sections of the pattern.

INSTRUCTIONS

Mother Cat
Right Front Leg
Work begins at the top of the right leg, which is at the top/center of the back. CO 8 sts provisionally onto 1 dpn. The upper leg portions of both legs are worked flat.

Row 1: P all sts.
Row 2: K all sts.
Row 3: P all sts.
Row 4: K all sts.
Row 5: P all sts.
Row 6: K1, M1L, K7. (9 sts)
Row 7: P all sts.
Row 8: K all sts.
Row 9: P all sts.

Row 10: K1, M1L, K8. (10 sts)
Row 11: P all sts.
Row 12: K all sts.
Row 13: P all sts.
Row 14: K1, M1L, K9. (11 sts)
Row 15: P all sts.
Row 16: K all sts.
Row 17: P all sts.
Row 18: K1, M1L, K10. (12 sts)
Row 19: P all sts.
Row 20: K all sts.
Row 21: P all sts.
Row 22: K1, M1L, K11. (13 sts)
Row 23: P all sts.
Row 24: K all sts.
Row 25: P all sts.
Row 26: K1, M1L, K12. (14 sts)
Row 27: P all sts.
Row 28: K all sts.
Row 29: P all sts.
Row 30: K1, M1L, K13. (15 sts)
Row 31: P all sts.
Row 32: K all sts.
Row 33: P all sts.
Row 34: K1, M1L, K14. (16 sts)
Row 35: P all sts.
Row 36: Slip 1, K9, turn work.
Row 37: Slip 1, P9, turn work.
Row 38: Slip 1, K9, turn work.
Row 39: Slip 1, P9.

Arrange these 10 sts evenly onto 2 dpns, and with RS together work a 3-needle bind-off (place remaining 6 sts on a third dpn by themselves). Turn work RS out.

Sts are now picked up on each side of the bind-off seam to begin the bottom of the leg. Beginning at the bind-off seam, pick up and knit the following 18 sts:

1st dpn: PU 6 sts along top edge from bind-off seam to live sts.
2nd dpn: K6.

3rd dpn: PU 6 sts along top edge from last live st to the bind-off seam.

Join sts in the round.

Rnds 1–3: K all sts.
Rnd 4: K2tog, K14, SSK. (16 sts)
Rnds 5–7: K all sts.
Rnd 8: K2tog, K12, SSK. (14 sts)
Rnds 9–11: K all sts.
Rnd 12: K2tog, K10, SSK. (12 sts)
Rnds 13–15: K all sts.
Rnd 16: K2tog, K8, SSK. (10 sts)
Rnds 17–24: K all sts.
Rnd 25: (K2, M1) 4 times, K2. (14 sts)
Rnds 26–29: K all sts.
Rnd 30: K9, w&t, P4, w&t, K5, w&t, P6, w&t, K10.

Cut yarn, thread through live sts, and pull closed. Use loose end to seam small hole at bottom of paw.

Left Front Leg

Remove the scrap yarn from the provisional CO sts of the right leg and place them onto a dpn. The left leg is worked directly from these 8 sts. With WS facing, rejoin working yarn at first st.

Row 1: P all sts.
Row 2: K all sts.
Row 3: P all sts.
Row 4: K all sts.
Row 5: P all sts.
Row 6: K7, M1R, K1. (9 sts)
Row 7: P all sts.
Row 8: K all sts.
Row 9: P all sts.

Row 10: K8, M1R, K1. (10 sts)
Row 11: P all sts.
Row 12: K all sts.
Row 13: P all sts.
Row 14: K9, M1R, K1. (11 sts)
Row 15: P all sts.
Row 16: K all sts.
Row 17: P all sts.
Row 18: K10, M1R, K1. (12 sts)
Row 19: P all sts.
Row 20: K all sts.
Row 21: P all sts.
Row 22: K11, M1R, K1. (13 sts)
Row 23: P all sts.
Row 24: K all sts.
Row 25: P all sts.
Row 26: K12, M1R, K1. (14 sts)
Row 27: P all sts.
Row 28: K all sts.
Row 29: P all sts.

Row 30: K13, M1R, K1. (15 sts)
Row 31: P all sts.
Row 32: K all sts.
Row 33: P all sts.
Row 34: K14, M1R, K1. (16 sts)
Row 35: P all sts.
Row 36: K all sts.
Row 37: Slip 1, P9, turn work.
Row 38: Slip 1, K9, turn work.
Row 39: Slip 1, P9, turn work.
Row 40: Slip 1, K9.

Arrange these 10 sts evenly onto 2 dpns, and with RS together work a 3-needle bind-off (place remaining 6 sts on a third dpn by themselves). Turn work RS out.

Sts are now picked up on each side of the bind-off seam to begin the bottom of the leg. Beginning at the bind-off seam, pick up and knit the following 18 sts:

1st dpn: PU 6 sts to the left of bind-off seam; join 6 live sts.
2nd dpn: K6.
3rd dpn: PU 6 sts from last live st to the bind-off seam.

Join sts in the round. Work the bottom of the left leg (Rnds 1–30) the same as the right leg.

Body

Setup: Sts are now picked up along the back edge of the upper legs to begin the body. With RS facing, begin at the top/center where the 2 legs are joined, and pick up the following 56 sts with 4 dpns:

1st dpn: PU 14 sts in 14 rows from top/center.
2nd dpn: PU the next 14 sts in the next 14 rows.

This should leave about 4 rows free before the lower leg where sts are joined in the round. The 2 legs are now brought together, and sts are picked up along the opposite edge the same way.

3rd dpn: PU 14 sts from 4 rows above lower left leg in next 14 rows.
4th dpn: PU the 14 sts in the next 14 rows, ending at top/center.

Join sts in the round; K28. This will be the new (temporary) EOR for Rows 1–10 only.

Row 1: K4, w&t, P8, w&t, K4.
Row 2: K6, w&t, P12, w&t, K6.
Row 3: K8 w&t, P16, w&t, K8.
Row 4: K10, w&t, P20, w&t, K10.
Row 5: K12, w&t, P24, w&t, K12.
Row 6: K14, w&t, P28, w&t, K14.
Row 7: K16, w&t, P32, w&t, K16.
Row 8: K18, w&t, P36, w&t, K18.
Row 9: K20, w&t, P40, w&t, K20.
Row 10: K22, w&t, P44, w&t, K22.
Row 11: K28 to original EOR.
Row 12: K all sts.
Row 13: K22, w&t, P44, w&t, K22.
Rnds 14–15: K all sts.

Repeat Row 13 and Rnds 14–15 nineteen more times for a total of 20 short rows and 40 knit rounds.

End of Body and Hole for Tail

Row 1: K18, w&t, P36, w&t, K18.
Row 2: K17, w&t, P34, w&t, K17.
Row 3: K16, w&t, P32, w&t, K16.
Row 4: K15, w&t, P30, w&t, K15.
Row 5: K14, w&t, P28, w&t, K14.
Row 6: K13, w&t, P26, w&t, K13.
Row 7: K12, w&t, P24, w&t, K9, place last 3 sts in rnd plus first 3 sts of next rnd onto a piece of scrap yarn, CO 3 new sts to EOR.
Row 8: CO 3 new sts to working needle, K8, w&t, P22, w&t, K11.
Row 9: K10, w&t, P20, w&t, K10.
Row 10: K9, w&t, P18, w&t, K9.
Row 11: K8, w&t, P16, w&t, K8.
Rnds 12–13: K all sts.

Place all live sts onto a piece of scrap yarn; cut yarn.

Bridge Between Legs

A small bridge, or tiny bit of fabric, is now worked to join the front legs. With RS facing, PU 4 sts along the inside edge of the joint on one of the legs. Work flat.

Row 1: P all sts.
Row 2: K all sts.
Row 3: P all sts.

Bind off, and then use loose end to seam to the opposite edge on the other leg and to the body in the back.

Head

Setup: Sts are now picked up around the front of the work to begin the head. Beginning at the top/center where the 2 legs are joined, pick up the following 60 sts with 4 dpns and RS facing:

1st dpn: PU 14 sts in about 19 rows (3 of every 4 rows) from top/center downward.
2nd dpn: PU 14 sts in the next 19 rows (3 of every 4 rows), and then PU 2 sts along the edge of the right side of the bridge.

Stitches are now picked up along the opposite edge the same way:

3rd dpn: PU 2 sts along the edge of the left side of the bridge, and then PU 14 sts in the next 19 rows (3 of every 4 rows).
4th dpn: PU 14 sts in the next 19 rows, ending at top/center.

Join sts in the round.

Rnd 1: (K2tog, K3) 12 times. (48 sts)
Rnds 2–4: K all sts.
Row 5: K6, w&t, P12, w&t, K6.
Row 6: K8, w&t, P16, w&t, K8.
Row 7: K10, w&t, P20, w&t, K10.
Row 8: K12, w&t, P24, w&t, K12.
Row 9: K14, w&t, P28, w&t, K14.
Row 10: K16, w&t, P32, w&t, K16.
Row 11: K18, w&t, P36, w&t, K18.
Row 12: K16, w&t, P32, w&t, K16.
Row 13: K14, w&t, P28, w&t, K14.
Row 14: K12, w&t, P24, w&t, K12.
Row 15: K10, w&t, P20, w&t, K10.
Rnd 16: K4, SSK, K2tog, K12, SSK, K4, K2tog, K12, SSK, K2tog, K4. (42 sts)
Rnd 17: K all sts.
Rnd 18: K3, SSK, K2tog, K10, SSK, K4, K2tog, K10, SSK, K2tog, K3. (36 sts)
Rnd 19: K all sts.

Rnd 20: K2, SSK, K2tog, K24, SSK, K2tog, K2. (32 sts)
Rnd 21: K all sts.
Rnd 22: K1, SSK, K2tog, K22, SSK, K2tog, K1. (28 sts)
Rnd 23: K all sts.
Rnd 24: SSK, K2tog, K20, SSK, K2tog. (24 sts)
Rnd 25: K all sts.
Rnd 26: (SSK) 6 times, (K2tog) 6 times. (12 sts)
Rnd 27: K all sts.
Rnd 28: (SSK) 3 times, (K2tog) 3 times. (6 sts)

Cut, thread through remaining live sts, and pull closed.

Tail

Setup: Place the 6 sts from scrap yarn onto 1 dpn. Sts are now picked up along the edge of the opening beneath them. Beginning at the bottom/center of the opening and with RS facing, PU/knit the following 18 sts:

1st dpn: PU 6 sts from bottom/center upward to the live sts.
2nd dpn: K6.
3rd dpn: PU 6 sts from the end of the live sts downward to the bottom/center.

Join in the round.

Rnds 1–10: K all sts.
Rnd 11: K2tog, K14, SSK. (16 sts)
Rnds 12–21: K all sts.
Rnd 22: K2tog, K12, SSK. (14 sts)
Rnds 23–32: K all sts.
Rnd 33: K2tog, K10, SSK. (12 sts)
Rnds 34–53: K all sts.

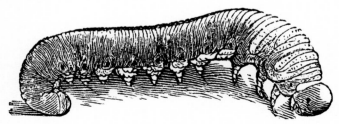

Rnd 54: K2tog, K8, SSK. (10 sts)
Rnds 55–64: K all sts.
Rnd 65: K2tog, K6, SSK. (8 sts)
Rnds 66–68: K all sts.

Cut yarn, thread through remaining live sts, and pull closed.

Lining

The body of the Potting Shed Cat is lined to provide a place for the kittens to be kept when not nursing and will hold up to 4 kittens. Place 56 sts from scrap yarn back onto 3 or 4 dpns. Join in the round.

Rnd 1: (K2tog, K5) 8 times. (48 sts)
Rnds 2–61: K all sts for 60 rounds.

This is the time to stuff your cat. The head, front legs, and tail are stuffed moderately; the body is stuffed slightly looser, leaving room for the lining and kittens to fit inside. After stuffing, continue with the rounds below to close the end of the lining.

Rnd 62: (K2tog, K4) 8 times. (40 sts)
Rnd 63: K all sts.
Rnd 64: (K2tog, K3) 8 times. (32 sts)
Rnd 65: K all sts.
Rnd 66: (K2tog, K2) 8 times. (24 sts)
Rnd 67: K all sts.
Rnd 68: (K2tog, K1) 8 times. (16 sts)
Rnd 69: K all sts.
Rnd 70: (K2tog) 8 times. (8 sts)

Cut yarn, thread through remaining live sts, and pull closed. Push lining and all rounds below the tail inside of body. After pushing in the lining, you'll need to shift the stuffing between the body and the lining around to make it even. To do this, insert a dpn from the outside into that space in several places, moving it back and forth to even out the stuffing.

Without kittens inside, your Potting Shed Cat's body should be more flat than round.

Nipples

Six nipples are embroidered with 1–2 yards of pink worsted weight yarn. These are placed along the short rows—3 on each side of the belly, and about 16 rows apart from each other. Make a floret going in a circle, with 8–10 "petals" each only about 1 stitch long. Pull needle up through the same hole in the center each time. Make a French knot in the center.

Ears (make 2 the same)

The ears are worked separately and seamed to head. Work begins at bottom of ear. With color A, CO 15 sts onto 3 dpns; join in the round.

Rnds 1–2: K all sts.
Rnd 3: K1, SSK, K2tog, K5, SSK, K2tog, K1. (11 sts)
Rnds 4–5: K all sts.
Rnd 6: SSK, K2tog, K3, SSK, K2tog. (7 sts)
Rnds 7–8: K all sts.

Cut yarn, thread through remaining live sts, pull closed. Flatten ears with the CO tail coming from one bottom corner. Bend slightly to create a slight hollowing in the front and seam to head at the first decrease on each side.

Back Legs (make 2 the same)

CO 9 sts onto 3 dpns, join in the round.

Rnd 1: K all sts.
Rnd 2: (M1, K1) 9 times. (18 sts)
Rnd 3: K all sts.
Rnd 4: (M1, K2) 9 times. (27 sts)
Rnd 5: K all sts.
Rnd 6: (M1, K3) 9 times. (36 sts)
Rnds 7–16: K all sts.
Rnd 17: K1, K2tog, K30, SSK, K1. (34 sts)
Rnds 18–19: K all sts.
Rnd 20: K1, K2tog, K28, SSK, K1. (32 sts)
Rnds 21–22: K all sts.
Rnd 23: K1, K2tog, K26, SSK, K1. (30 sts)
Rnds 24–25: K all sts.
Rnd 26: K1, K2tog, K24, SSK, K1. (28 sts)
Rnds 27–28: K all sts.

Rnd 29: K1, K2tog, K22, SSK, K1. (26 sts)
Rnds 30–31: K all sts.
Rnd 32: K1, K2tog, K20, SSK, K1. (24 sts)
Rnds 33–34: K all sts.
Rnd 35: K1, K2tog, K18, SSK, K1. (22 sts)
Rnds 36–37: K all sts.
Rnd 38: K1, K2tog, K16, SSK, K1. (20 sts)
Rnds 39–40: K all sts.
Rnd 41: K1, K2tog, K14, SSK, K1. (18 sts)
Rnds 42–43: K all sts.
Rnd 44: K1, K2tog, K12, SSK, K1. (16 sts)
Rnds 45–46: K all sts.
Rnd 47: K1, K2tog, K10, SSK, K1. (14 sts)
Rnds 48–49: K all sts.
Row 50: K5, turn work.
Row 51: Slip 1, P9, turn work.

Place these 10 sts onto 1 dpn, and the 4 other sts onto a separate dpn.

Row 52: Slip 1, K9, turn work.
Row 53: Slip 1, P9, turn work.
Row 54: Slip 1, K9, turn work.

Arrange these 10 sts onto 2 dpns. Place RS together and work a 3-needle bind-off. Turn work RS out.

Sts are now picked up around the opening that was just created to begin the bottom of the leg. Beginning at the bind-off seam, pick up and knit the following 16 sts:

1st dpn: PU 6 sts along top edge from bind-off seam to live sts.
2nd dpn: K4.
3rd dpn: PU 6 sts along top edge from live sts to the bind-off seam.

Join in the round.

Rnd 1: K all sts.
Rnd 2: K2tog, K12, SSK. (14 sts)
Rnd 3: K all sts.
Rnd 4: K2tog, K10, SSK. (12 sts)
Rnd 5: K all sts.
Rnd 6: K2tog, K8, SSK. (10 sts)
Rnds 7–14: K all sts.

Rnd 15: (K2, M1) 4 times, K2. (14 sts)
Rnds 16–19: K all sts.
Rnd 20: K9, w&t, P4, w&t, K5, w&t, P6, w&t, K10.

Stuff leg while still on the needles. Stuff the upper part loosely—it should be more flat than round; stuff bottom fully. Then cut yarn, thread through live sts, and pull closed. Use loose end to seam small hole at bottom of paw.

Position back legs on your cat as pictured, with top of leg about 5 in./12.5 cm from end and pointing backwards and down. Seam upper leg to body about 0.5 in./1.5 cm from the edge around all parts that are touching the body. Legs can be placed at different angles to create a more natural look, if desired.

Finishing

The upper front leg can be accentuated by making a 2 in./5 cm running stitch on either side of it and pulling a little to cinch slightly together. Front legs can be left as they are or tacked to the body in any position.

Kitten

NOTES

- The striped kitten is made with 2 rnds of color A alternated with 1 rnd of color B.
- The spots on the calico kitten's body were made with intarsia in random locations; the tail was striped, and the spots on the head were embroidered after stuffing.
- The kitten's front and back legs are left unstuffed and will be wonky, much like those of a real newborn kitten. They are made to bend in any direction.

Body

Work begins at neckline. CO 16 sts onto 3 dpns; join sts in the round.

Rnds 1–6: K all sts.
Rnd 7: (K4, M1L, K2, M1R) 2 times, K4. (20 sts)
Rnds 8–13: K all sts.
Rnd 14: (K4, SSK, K2tog) 2 times, K4. (16 sts)
Rnds 15–18: K all sts.

Row 19: K2, w&t, P4, w&t, K2.

Row 20: K4, w&t, P8, w&t, K4.

Row 21: K6, w&t, P12, w&t, K5, place last st in rnd plus first st in next rnd on a piece of scrap yarn, CO 1 new st to EOR.

Row 22: CO 1 new st to working needle, K1, w&t, P4, w&t, K2.

Row 23: K4, w&t, P8, w&t, K4.

Back Right Leg

Setup: K8, place remaining 8 on scrap yarn. Arrange first 8 on 3 dpns and join them in the round.

Rnds 1–2: K all sts.

Rnd 3: K2tog, K4, SSK. (6 sts)

Rnds 4–5: K all sts.

Rnd 6: K2, w&t, P2, w&t, K3, w&t, P4, w&t, K1 (EOR).

Rnd 7: K2tog, K2, SSK all on 1 dpn. (4 sts)

Rows 8–11: Work 4 rows of a 4-st I-cord—without turning, slide the stitches to the other end of the needle and pull up the working yarn from the last stitch to start the next row.

Cut yarn, thread through live sts, and pull closed. Weave in loose end.

Back Left Leg

Setup: Place 8 sts from scrap yarn onto a dpn. With RS facing, rejoin working yarn at first st leaving a 6-inch tail for seaming; K8. Arrange sts on 3 dpns and join in the round.

Rnds 1–2: K all sts.

Rnd 3: K2tog, K4, SSK. (6 sts)

Rnds 4–5: K all sts.

Rnd 6: W&t, P2, w&t, K3, w&t, P4, w&t, K3 (EOR).

Rnd 7: K2tog, K2, SSK all on 1 dpn. (4 sts)

Rows 8–11: Work 4 rows of a 4-st I-cord.

Cut yarn, thread through live sts, and pull closed. Weave in loose end.

The kitten's body can be stuffed at this point. Seam hole between legs closed from front to back.

Tail

Setup: Place 2 live sts from scrap yarn onto 1 dpn. Beginning at the bottom/center of the opening beneath the live sts, PU/knit the following 6 sts with RS facing and 3 dpns:

1st dpn: PU 2 sts along edge from bottom/center of hole to live sts.
2nd dpn: K2.
3rd dpn: PU 2 sts along edge from live sts to bottom/center of hole.

Rnds 1–2: K all sts.
Rnd 3: K2tog, K2, SSK all on 1 dpn. (4 sts)

The remaining rows are all worked as an I-cord.

Rows 4–5: K all sts.
Row 6: K2tog, K2. (3 sts)
Rows 7–8: K all sts.
Row 9: K2tog, K1. (2 sts)
Rows 10–11: K all sts.

Cut yarn, thread through remaining live sts, and pull closed. Weave in loose end.

Head

With RS facing and 3 dpns, begin at back/center of neck and PU 16 sts, 1 st in each of the original CO sts. Join in the round.

Rnd 1: K all sts.
Rnd 2: (M1, K1) 4 times, K8, (M1, K1) 4 times. (24 sts)
Rnd 3: K all sts.
Rnd 4: K2, SSK, K2tog, K12, SSK, K2tog, K2. (20 sts)
Rnd 5: K all sts.
Rnd 6: K1, SSK, K2tog, K10, SSK, K2tog, K1. (16 sts)
Rnd 7: K all sts.
Rnd 8: SSK, K2tog, K8, SSK, K2tog. (12 sts)
Rnd 9: K all sts.

Stuff head now.

Rnd 10: (SSK) 3 times, (K2tog) 3 times. (6 sts)

Cut yarn, thread through remaining live sts, and pull closed. Weave in loose end.

Eyes are embroidered as small straight lines with black yarn. A tiny nose, the width of 1 st, is embroidered with pink yarn.

Front Legs (make 2 the same)

The kitten's front legs are worked separately and seamed to body. CO 8 sts onto 3 dpns and join in the round.

Rnds 1–2: K all sts.
Rnd 3: K2tog, K4, SSK. (6 sts)
Rnds 4–5: K all sts.
Rnd 6: K1, w&t, P2, w&t, K3, w&t, P4, w&t, K2 (EOR).
Row 7: K2tog, K2, SSK all on 1 dpn. (4 sts)
Rows 8–11: Work 4 rows of a 4-st I-cord.

Seam to belly of kitten in line with the back legs and 3 rows from the original CO sts.

Ears (make 2 the same)

CO 5 sts onto 1 dpn. Work all 3 rows below as an I-cord, pulling up yarn from the last st.

Row 1: K all sts.
Row 2: SSK, K1, K2tog. (3 sts)
Row 3: K3tog. (1 st)

Cut yarn and pull through last st. Weave loose end down one side. Seam ears to head with the CO tail at first decrease st on each side; face the back side forward since it will be slightly open.

Aunt Pru is Mr. Morgan's aunt and Granddad's younger sister. She came to live with her nephew and his family eight years ago to help Mrs. Morgan care for the twins after they were born. This was her idea and seemed like a good one to everyone at the time, but she hadn't any experience with babies or children and things were awkward between her and Winnifred. She settled into her room and unpacked a large trunk filled with several of what appeared to be the same black dress. No one has dared to bring up the subject of her leaving.

Aunt Pru was never married, although it's rumoured she had a beau while she was in finishing school. She has her father's aquiline nose and belongs, as her mother did, to the local temperance society. She records all births and deaths in the Morgan family Bible with a grave sense of responsibility.

Aunt Pru pampers and adores her Persian cat, which she brought with her when she moved into the house and which the children are not allowed to pester—her word. The gossip in the servants' quarters is that the Persian's hair has been found in Aunt Pru's own hairbrush on many occasions.

Aunt Pru's
Persian

FINISHED SIZE

- 12 in./30.5 cm tall
- 7 in./18 cm wide
- 10 in./25.5 cm deep (not including tail)

YARN

Woolfolk Flette Bulky Yarn: 140 yd./128 m total

- White cat: Color FB00
- Light gray cat: Color FB01
- Dark gray cat: Color FB05

NEEDLES

- US size 5/3.75 mm straight needles
- US size 5/3.75 mm double-pointed needles

NOTE

The increases in the paws and tail are worked as "CO 1," which refers to the backwards loop method of casting on a stitch to the working needle. If using the recommended yarn or another yarn such as eyelash, this is the best increase to use. However, if using a plain, non-hairy or non-furry yarn, this increase may leave a hole, so any other can be substituted.

INSTRUCTIONS

Chest

CO 28 sts *loosely* onto 1 straight needle.

Row 1 (WS): P all sts.
Row 2 (RS): K all sts.

Repeat Rows 1–2 fourteen more times for a total of 30 rows worked in stockinette stitch, and then work Row 1 one more time.

Legs (work both the same)

Setup: K14, place remaining 14 sts on a piece of scrap yarn. Arrange 14 sts just knit onto 3 dpns; join in the round.

Rnds 1–16: K all sts.
Rnd 17: K5, (CO 1, K2) 2 times, CO 1, K5. (17 sts)
Rnd 18: K all sts.
Rnd 19: K11, w&t, P4, w&t, K5, w&t, P6, w&t, K11 (EOR).

Cut yarn, thread through live sts, and pull closed. Weave in loose end. Stuffing the legs at this point is recommended.

Body

Setup: Hold first and last CO sts together to form a circle—this will become the neck opening. Seam

together the top 3 rows. Sts are now picked up along the edges of the chest and across the top of the legs to shape the beginning of the body.

Begin at the top/center of opening (just below the 3 rows that were seamed together). With RS facing, pick up the following number of stitches evenly with 3 dpns:

1st dpn: PU 24 sts from the top/center of opening down to the right leg seam.
2nd dpn: PU 8 sts across the bottom of the opening from the right leg seam to the left leg seam.
3rd dpn: PU 24 sts from the left leg seam up to the top/center of opening.

This creates a total of 56 body sts, which are then joined in the round. These can be rearranged on 3 or 4 dpns or transferred to a circular needle as you proceed with the body.

Rnds 1–2: K all sts.
Row 3: K10, w&t, P20, w&t, K10.
Rnd 4: K all sts.
Row 5: K12, w&t, P24, w&t, K12.
Rnd 6: K all sts.
Row 7: K14, w&t, P28, w&t, K14.
Rnd 8: K all sts.
Row 9: K16, w&t, P32, w&t, K16.
Rnd 10: K all sts.
Row 11: K18, w&t, P36, w&t, K18.

Rnd 12: K all sts.
Row 13: K8, w&t, P16, w&t, K8.
Row 14: K9, w&t, P18, w&t, K9.
Row 15: K10, w&t, P20, w&t, K10.
Row 16: K11, w&t, P22, w&t, K11.
Row 17: K12, w&t, P24, w&t, K12.
Row 18: K13, w&t, P26, w&t, K13.
Row 19: K14, w&t, P28, w&t, K14.
Row 20: K15, w&t, P30, w&t, K15.
Row 21: K16, w&t, P32, w&t, K16.
Row 22: K17, w&t, P34, w&t, K17.
Row 23: K18, w&t, P36, w&t, K18.
Row 24: K19, w&t, P38, w&t, K19.
Row 25: K20, w&t, P40, w&t, K20.
Rnd 26: K all sts.
Rnd 27: K52, place the last 4 sts in the round plus the first 4 sts from the next round onto 1 piece of scrap yarn, CO 4 new sts to EOR.
Rnd 28: CO 4 new sts to working needle, K52.
Rnds 29–38: K all sts.

Cut yarn; place all sts on piece of scrap yarn. The base of the cat will be worked last.

Head

Sts are now picked up in and around the original CO sts to begin the head.

Setup: Begin at the first CO st (back/center of opening). With RS facing, pick up the following number of stitches evenly with 3 dpns. ***Note:*** This will be more sts than the original CO number, so you'll need to pick up additional strands of yarn between the CO sts in order to come up with the right number.

1st dpn: PU 12 sts from the first CO st along left side of neck.

2nd dpn: PU 14 sts across the front of the opening (make sure to center these with the front of the body/chest).

3rd dpn: PU 12 sts along right side of neck to the EOR. (38 sts)

Join sts in the round.

Rnds 1–3: K all sts.

Note: The following round contains multiple short rows that will create 2 "bumps," one on each side of and below where the nose will be.

Rnd 4: K17, w&t, P6, w&t, K5, w&t, P4, w&t, K13, w&t, P6, w&t, K5, w&t, P4, w&t, K18 (EOR).

Rnd 5: K17, SSK, K2tog, K17. (36 sts)

Rnds 6–9: K all sts.

Rnd 10: (K2tog, K4) 6 times. (30 sts)

Rnd 11: K all sts.

Rnd 12: (K2tog, K3) 6 times. (24 sts)

Rnd 13: K all sts.

Rnd 14: (K2tog, K2) 6 times. (18 sts)

Rnd 15: K all sts.

Rnd 16: (K2tog, K1) 6 times. (12 sts)

Cut yarn, thread through remaining live sts; pull closed. Weave in loose end.

Tail

Setup: Place 8 live sts from scrap yarn onto 1 dpn. Sts are now picked up on either side of these live sts. With RS facing, begin in the bottom/center of opening beneath the tail and PU the following sts with 2 additional dpns:

1st dpn: PU 6 sts from bottom/center of opening along left edge up to the live sts.

2nd dpn: K8.

3rd dpn: PU 6 sts from live sts along right edge down to bottom/center of opening. (20 sts)

Rnds 1–26: K all sts.

Rnd 27: (K5, CO 1) 4 times. (24 sts)

Rnds 28–42: K all sts.

Rnd 43: (K2tog, K4) 4 times. (20 sts)

Rnd 44: K all sts.

Rnd 45: (K2tog, K3) 4 times. (16 sts)

Rnd 46: K all sts.

Cut yarn, thread through remaining live sts, and pull closed. Weave in loose end.

If using safety eyes and/or safety nose, position and attach them now. The nose will go in the center between and slightly above the 2 bumps that were created by short rows. Stuff head, tail, and legs now. It's easier to knit the base if the body is left unstuffed at this point.

Base

Setup: Place the 56 sts from scrap yarn onto 3 or 4 dpns.

Rnd 1: (K2tog, K5) 8 times. (48 sts)
Rnd 2: K all sts.
Rnd 3: (K2tog, K4) 8 times. (40 sts)
Rnd 4: K all sts.
Rnd 5: (K2tog, K3) 8 times. (32 sts)
Rnd 6: K all sts.
Rnd 7: (K2tog, K2) 8 times. (24 sts)
Rnd 8: K all sts.

Stuff the remainder of the body at this time. Stuff all areas fully, using a dpn from the outside to shift stuffing evenly around and where you want it to go.

Rnd 9: (K2tog, K1) 8 times. (16 sts)
Rnd 10: K all sts.
Rnd 11: (K2tog) 8 times. (8 sts)

Cut yarn, thread through remaining live sts; pull closed. Weave in loose end. The base of your Persian should be flattened so that the fullness of the body comes all the way down.

Ears (make 2 the same)

CO 12 sts onto 3 dpns; join in the round.

Rnds 1–4: K all sts.
Rnd 5: (K1, SSK, K2tog, K1) 2 times. (8 sts)
Rnd 6: K all sts.

Cut yarn, thread through remaining live sts, and pull closed. Weave in loose end. Position both ears atop head and use CO tail to seam in place.

Finishing

The 2 bumps on either side of the nose are accentuated with a piece of yarn that runs beneath them and is pulled tightly. Insert darning needle with a piece of yarn up through fabric right below the nose. Encircle the bottom half of a bump with the yarn, going down into the fabric on the far end of the bump and then back up through where the nose will be; pull to tighten and repeat on the other side.

Tail can be tacked alongside of body; front paws can be seamed together.

The Morgan children have a dollhouse in the nursery, which over the years has accumulated an abundance of dolls, furnishings, and household accessories. Emily has made tiny, braided rugs and needlepointed cushions for the bedrooms. The twins have painted miniature artwork for the walls, and Mrs. Morgan, being a knitter, came up with a tiny knitting pattern modeled after the cat who lives in their own parlour.

Tiny
Parlour
Cat

FINISHED SIZE
- 2.5 in./6.5 cm long (not including tail)
- 1.5 in./4 cm wide

YARN
Gedifra Laura: 20 yd./18.5 cm total
- Gray cat: Color 3206 (A); Color 3201 (B)
- Orange cat: Color 3214 (A); Color 3201 (B)
- Black cat: Color 3207 (A); Color 3201 (B)

Note: Although this yarn is classified as Aran weight on Ravelry, it is barely fingering weight when knitted for a stuffed animal. If looking for a substitute yarn to use on this project, please keep that point in mind.

NEEDLES
- US size 1/2.25 mm double-pointed needles

INSTRUCTIONS

Body

Work begins at a vertical line between chest and body. CO 18 sts onto 3 dpns and join in the round.

Rnds 1–2: K all sts.
Rnd 3: K1, M1R, K16, M1L, K1. (20 sts)
Rnds 4–5: K all sts.
Rnd 6: K1, M1R, K18, M1L, K1. (22 sts)
Rnds 7–8: K all sts.
Rnd 9: K1, M1R, K2, M1R, K16, M1L, K2, M1L, K1. (26 sts)

Rnds 10–17: K all sts.
Rnd 18: K1, (K2tog, K2) 2 times, K2tog, K4, (SSK, K2) 2 times, SSK, K1. (20 sts)
Rnd 19: K all sts.
Rnd 20: (K2tog, K1) 2 times, K2tog, K4, (SSK, K1) 2 times, SSK. (14 sts)
Rnd 21: K all sts.
Rnd 22: (K2tog) 3 times, K2, (SSK) 3 times. (8 sts)
Rnd 23: K all sts.
Rnd 24: K2tog, K4, SSK (all on 1 dpn). (6 sts)

Tail

Work 22 rows of a 6-st I-cord—without turning, slide the stitches to the other end of the needle and pull up the working yarn from the last stitch to start the next row. Then (K2tog) 3 times. Cut yarn, thread through remaining live sts, and pull closed. Weave in loose end.

Stuff fully, flattening the bottom of the cat. Keep in mind that the increases and decreases are on the top.

Chest

Sts are now picked up in the original CO sts to work the chest. Locate the first CO st and count 9 sts to the left. This should be directly across from the first CO st, at the bottom/center of the body.

With color B, PU 1 st in the 9th st and 1 more in the next CO stitch. (2 sts)

Turn work now and at the end of each of the following rows.

Row 1: P2, PUP1. (3 sts)
Row 2: K3, PU1. (4 sts)
Row 3: P4, PUP1. (5 sts)
Row 4: K5, PU1. (6 sts)
Row 5: P6, PUP1. (7 sts)
Row 6: K7, PU1. (8 sts)
Row 7: P8, PUP1. (9 sts)
Row 8: K9, PU1. (10 sts)
Row 9: P10, PUP1. (11 sts)
Row 10: K11, PU1, cut color B; join color A, PU 3 (EOR). (15 sts)

Head

Rnd 1: PU 3 sts in the remaining CO sts, K15. (18 sts)
Rnd 2: K3, (K2tog) 3 times, (SSK) 3 times, K3. (12 sts)
Rnds 3–4: K all sts.
Rnd 5: K3, M1L, K1, M1R, K4, M1L, K1, M1R, K3. (16 sts)
Rnds 6–10: K all sts.

Stuff chest and head fully now.

Ears

1. K1, place it on a piece of scrap yarn.
2. Slip next 6 sts onto a dpn without knitting them.
3. Slip all remaining sts in round (9) onto a piece of scrap yarn.
4. Arrange 6 sts that are currently on the dpn onto 3 dpns and join in the round.
5. K 2 rnds.
6. (K2tog) 3 times.
7. Cut yarn, leaving a tail of about 12 in./30.5 cm for working second ear.
8. Thread it through remaining 3 sts and pull closed.
9. Weave tail down left side of ear, seaming it closed if needed.
10. Slip tail through next 2 sts from scrap yarn.

11. Arrange next 6 sts onto 3 dpns; join in the round.
12. Repeat steps 5, 6, and 8.
13. Weave loose end down right side of ear, seaming it closed if needed.
14. Slip last 2 sts from scrap yarn onto loose end.
15. Pull to cinch all 4 center sts closed.

Legs (make 2 the same)

CO 6 sts onto 1 dpn. Work 10 rows of a 6-st I-cord. Cut yarn, thread through live sts, and pull closed. Weave in loose end. Seam to the bottom of cat side by side with about half sticking out in front of chest.

Mr. Henry Morgan is a man who is hard to know completely. To people outside of his home, he is known to be quiet, head down and focused intently on work in his actuarial position in the city. At home, another side of him is known—he's a horse for the twins on his hands and knees, he's a writer of Petrarchan sonnets, and he loves to cook.

Cook has every other Tuesday off, so on those days Mr. Morgan trades his top hat for an apron and spends all afternoon in the kitchen. He is not a fancy or complicated cook and makes the same two or three dishes over and over, but he enjoys doing it and tells his family that he could have been a professional chef.

The cat who calls himself Mr. Morgan's is a feisty ginger who won't tolerate anyone but his owner and has gotten into loud hissing fights with most of the cats in the house. Mr. Morgan and his cat are two of the most opposite souls on earth, and yet somehow they get along swimmingly.

The
Gentleman's
Ginger

FINISHED SIZE

- 13 in./33 cm tall at highest point
- 15 in./38 cm long from head to tail

YARN

Berroco Vintage Chunky: 320 yd./292.5 m total
(color A/main color: 270 yd./247 m; color B/paws: 20
yd./18.5 m; color C/optional stripes: 30 yd./27.5 m)

- Cat 1: 61192 Marmalade (A); 6100 Snow Day (B)
- Cat 2: 6176 Pumpkin (A); 6100 Snow Day (B)
- Cat 3: 61192 Marmalade (A); 6100
  Snow Day (B); 6176 Pumpkin (C)

NEEDLES

- US size 5/3.75 mm double-pointed needles

INSTRUCTIONS

Right Front Leg

Work begins at top/center of neck. With color A,
CO 4 sts provisionally onto 1 dpn. The upper part
of each leg is worked flat. When casting on a new
stitch to the working needle, use the backwards loop
cast on.

Row 1 and all odd rows: P all sts.
Row 2: K all sts.
Row 4: CO 1 st to working needle, K4. (5 sts)
Row 6: CO 1 st to working needle, K5. (6 sts)
Row 8: CO 1 st to working needle, K6. (7 sts)
Row 10: CO 1 st to working needle, K7. (8 sts)
Row 12: CO 1 st to working needle, K8. (9 sts)
Row 14: CO 1 st to working needle, K9. (10 sts)
Row 16: CO 1 st to working needle, K10. (11 sts)
Row 18: CO 1 st to working needle, K11. (12 sts)
Row 20: CO 1 st to working needle, K12. (13 sts)
Row 22: CO 1 st to working needle, K13. (14 sts)
Row 24: CO 1 st to working needle, K14, CO 1 st
to EOR. (16 sts)
Row 26: CO 1 st to working needle, K16, CO 1 st
to EOR. (18 sts)
Row 28: CO 1 st to working needle, K18, CO 1 st
to EOR. (20 sts)

Arrange sts on 3 dpns, join in the round.

Row 29: K10, turn work.

Row 30: Slip 1, P7, turn work.
Row 31: Slip 1, K7.

Arrange these 8 sts on 2 dpns, and with RS sides
facing work a 3-needle bind-off. Cut yarn and pull
through last st. Turn work RS out again.

Sts are now picked up on both sides of the 3-needle
bind-off to work the lower part of the leg. With RS
facing, begin at the bind-off seam and pick up or knit
the following sts with 3 dpns:

1st dpn: PU 4 sts from bind-off seam to live sts.
2nd dpn: K the 12 live sts.
3rd dpn: PU 4 sts from live sts to bind-off seam
(EOR). (20 sts)

Sts are joined in the round.

Note: If working optional stripes with color C, use it
for Rnds 5, 6, 11, 12, 17, 18, 23, and 24.

Rnds 1–3: K all sts.
Rnd 4: K2tog, K16, SSK. (18 sts)
Rnds 5–8: K all sts.
Rnd 9: K2tog, K14, SSK. (16 sts)

Rnds 10–14: K all sts.
Rnd 15: K2tog, K12, SSK. (14 sts)
Rnds 16–21: K all sts.
Rnd 22: K2tog, K10, SSK. (12 sts)
Rnds 23–32: K all sts.

Switch to color B to work the paw (optional).

Rnd 33: K3, (M1, K1) 6 times, K3. (18 sts)
Rnd 34: K all sts.

The following round contains multiple short rows within it. Work exactly as written.

Rnd 35: K11, w&t, P4, w&t, K5, w&t, P6, w&t, K12.
Rnd 36: (K2tog, K1) 6 times. (12 sts)

Cut yarn, thread through remaining live sts, and pull closed. Use loose end to seam hole at bottom of paw closed.

Left Front Leg

Work directly from the CO sts of the right leg. Unravel the scrap yarn used for the provisional cast-on, placing live sts onto 1 dpn as you do. Rejoin color A at first st on purl side of work.

Row 1 and all odd rows through Row 27: P all sts.
Row 2: K all sts.
Row 4: K4, CO 1 to EOR. (5 sts)
Row 6: K5, CO 1 to EOR. (6 sts)
Row 8: K6, CO 1 to EOR. (7 sts)
Row 10: K7, CO 1 to EOR. (8 sts)
Row 12: K8, CO 1 to EOR. (9 sts)
Row 14: K9, CO 1 to EOR. (10 sts)
Row 16: K10, CO 1 to EOR. (11 sts)
Row 18: K11, CO 1 to EOR. (12 sts)
Row 20: K12, CO 1 to EOR. (13 sts)

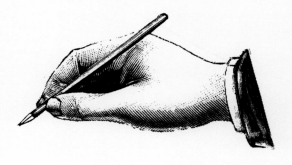

Row 22: K13, CO 1 to EOR. (14 sts)
Row 24: CO 1 to working needle, K14, CO 1 to EOR. (16 sts)
Row 26: CO 1 to working needle, K16, CO 1 to EOR. (18 sts)
Row 28: CO 1 to working needle, K18, CO 1 to EOR. (20 sts)

Arrange sts on 3 dpns, join in the round.

Row 29: K18, turn work.
Row 30: Slip 1, P7, turn work.
Row 31: Slip 1, K7.

Arrange these 8 sts on 2 dpns and with RS facing work a 3-needle bind-off. Cut yarn and pull through last st. Turn work RS out again. The remainder of the left leg is worked the same as the right. Legs and paws can be stuffed now.

Body

Stitches are now picked up along the back edge of the legs to begin the body. With RS facing and 4 dpns, begin at the top/center where legs are joined and PU the following stitches along the back edge of the right leg—1 st in every 1 row:

1st dpn: PU 14 sts from top/center down edge of right leg.
2nd dpn: PU 14 sts down to where leg sts are joined in the round.

Bring legs together and begin picking up sts on the left leg. **Note:** Although legs are brought together at this point, they will be separated slightly in the end, which is ideal.

3rd dpn: PU 14 sts from where leg sts are joined in the round upward.
4th dpn: PU 14 sts to top/center. (56 sts)

K28 sts to the bottom/center of sts. This will be the EOR for the first set of short rows. These short rows will shape the bottom/front of your cat and change the direction of work.

Row 1: K4, w&t, P8, w&t, K4.
Row 2: K6, w&t, P12, w&t, K6.

Row 3: K8, w&t, P16, w&t, K8.
Row 4: K10, w&t, P20, w&t, K10.
Row 5: K12, w&t, P24, w&t, K12.
Row 6: K14, w&t P28, w&t, K14.
Row 7: K16, w&t, P32, w&t, K16.
Row 8: K18, w&t, P36, w&t, K18.
Row 9: K20, w&t, P40, w&t, K20.
Row 10: K22, w&t, P44, w&t, K50 to original top/ center (EOR).

The body of the cat is worked in several short row "wedges" that shape the arch, accompanied by 2 knit rounds.

Note: If working optional stripes with color C, use it for Rows 9, 15, and 21.

Rnd 1: K1, M1, K54, M1, K1. (58 sts)
Rnd 2: K all sts.
Row 3: K18, w&t, P36, w&t, K18.
Row 4: K20, w&t, P40, w&t, K20.
Row 5: K22, w&t, P44, w&t, K22.
Row 6: K24, w&t, P48, w&t, K24.
Rnd 7: K1, M1, K56, M1, K1. (60 sts)

Rnd 8: K all sts.
Row 9: K19, w&t, P38, w&t, K19.
Row 10: K21, w&t, P42, w&t, K21.
Row 11: K23, w&t, P46, w&t, K23.
Row 12: K25, w&t, P50, w&t, K25.
Rnd 13: K1, M1, K58, M1, K1. (62 sts)
Rnd 14: K all sts.
Row 15: K20, w&t, P40, w&t, K20.
Row 16: K22, w&t, P44, w&t, K22.
Row 17: K24, w&t, P48, w&t, K24.
Row 18: K26, w&t, P52, w&t, K26.
Rnd 19: K1, M1, K60, M1, K1. (64 sts)
Rnd 20: K all sts.
Row 21: K21, w&t, P42, w&t, K21. (Cut optional stripe color.)
Row 22: K23, w&t, P46, w&t, K23.
Row 23: K25, w&t, P50, w&t, K25.
Row 24: K27, w&t, P54, w&t, K27.
Rnds 25–26: K all sts.

Repeat Rows/Rnds 21–26 three more times for a total of 7 wedges. On the last knit round, stop after

Rnd 25 (do not work Rnd 26). Replace it with the Rnd 26 below to leave a hole for the tail stitches.

Rnd 26: K60, place last 4 sts in rnd plus first 4 sts of next rnd onto a small piece of scrap yarn, CO 4 new sts to the EOR. (60 sts)

Rnd 27: CO 4 new sts to working needle, K60. (64 sts)

The following set of short rows will form the fabric beneath the tail and between legs.

Row 28: K5, w&t, P10, w&t, K5.
Row 29: K6, w&t, P12, w&t, K6.
Row 30: K7, w&t, P14, w&t, K7.
Row 31: K8, w&t, P16, w&t, K8.
Row 32: K9, w&t, P18, w&t, K9.
Row 33: K10, w&t, P20, w&t, K10.
Row 34: K11, w&t, P22, w&t, K11.
Row 35: K12, w&t, P24, w&t, K12.
Row 36: K13, w&t, P26, w&t, K13.
Row 37: K14, w&t, P28, w&t, K14.

Cut yarn. Place 64 live sts onto a piece of scrap yarn.

Tail

Sts are now picked up around the edge of the opening below the 8 live sts to work the tail. With RS facing, begin at the bottom/center of opening and PU/knit the following sts with 3 dpns before joining in the round:

1st dpn: PU 6 sts from bottom/center of opening to live sts at top.
2nd dpn: K8 live sts.
3rd dpn: PU 6 sts from last live st to bottom/center of opening (EOR).

Note: If working optional stripes with color C, use it for Rnds 16, 17, 23, 24, 30, and 31.

Rnds 1–10: K all sts.
Rnd 11: K1, M1, K18, M1, K1. (22 sts)
Rnds 12–21: K all sts.
Rnd 22: K1, M1, K20, M1, K1. (24 sts)
Rnds 23–32: K all sts.
Rnd 33: K1, M1, K22, M1, K1. (26 sts)
Rnds 34–53: K all sts.
Rnd 54: K2tog, K22, SSK. (24 sts)
Rnd 55: K all sts.
Rnd 56: (K2tog, K2) 6 times. (18 sts)
Rnds 57–59: K all sts.

Cut yarn, thread through remaining live sts, and pull closed.

Bridge Between Front Legs

With color B, RS facing, and 1 dpn, PU 4 sts between front legs. Begin with a purl row and work a total of 7 rows in stockinette stitch. Bind off, cut yarn leaving a tail of 8–10 in./20.5–25.5 cm to seam sides of bridge to inner legs.

Head

Sts are now picked up clockwise along the edge of the front legs and across the bridge to work the head. With color A and RS facing, begin at the top/center and pick up the following sts with 4 dpns.

1st dpn: PU 12 sts from top/center downward.
2nd dpn: PU 12 sts from 1st dpn down to bottom/center.
3rd dpn: PU 12 sts from bottom/center upward.
4th dpn: PU 12 sts up to top/center (EOR). (48 sts)

Join sts in the round.

Rnd 1: K21, SSK, K2, K2tog, K21. (46 sts)
Rnd 2: K all sts.
Rnd 3: K20, SSK, K2, K2tog, K20. (44 sts)
Rnd 4: K all sts.
Rnd 5: K5, (M1, K2) 4 times, K6, SSK, K2, K2tog, K6, (K2, M1) 4 times, K5. (50 sts)
Rnd 6: K all sts.
Rnd 7: K8, (M1, K2) 4 times, K6, SSK, K2, K2tog, K6, (K2, M1) 4 times, K8. (56 sts)
Rnd 8: K all sts.
Rnd 9: K5, SSK, K2tog, K16, SSK, K2, K2tog, K16, SSK, K2tog, K5. (50 sts)
Rnd 10: K all sts.
Rnd 11: K4, SSK, K2tog, K14, SSK, K2, K2tog, K14, SSK, K2tog, K4. (44 sts)
Rnd 12: K all sts.

Rnd 13: K3, SSK, K2tog, K30, SSK, K2tog, K3. (40 sts)
Rnd 14: K all sts.
Rnd 15: K2, SSK, K2tog, K28, SSK, K2tog, K2. (36 sts)
Rnd 16: K all sts.
Rnd 17: K1, SSK, K2tog, K26, SSK, K2tog, K1. (32 sts)
Rnd 18: K all sts.
Rnd 19: SSK, K2tog, K24, SSK, K2tog. (28 sts)
Rnd 20: K all sts.
Rnd 21: (SSK) 7 times, (K2tog) 7 times. (14 sts)
Rnd 22: K all sts.
Rnd 23: (SSK) 3 times, K2, (K2tog) 3 times. (8 sts)

Cut yarn, thread through remaining live sts, and pull closed. Stuff front legs, head, and tail now. Leave the body unstuffed.

Right Back Leg

Place the first 32 sts from scrap yarn onto 3 dpns. Leave remaining 32 sts on scrap yarn. Rejoin color A at first st, K32. Join sts in the round and K26 (new EOR).

Note: If working optional stripes with color C, use it for Rnds 9, 10, 17, 18, 25, and 26.

Rnds 1–3: K all sts.
Rnd 4: K2tog, K28, SSK. (30 sts)
Rnds 5–7: K all sts.
Rnd 8: K2tog, K26, SSK. (28 sts)
Rnds 9–10: K all sts.
Rnd 11: K2tog, K24, SSK. (26 sts)
Rnds 12–13: K all sts.
Rnd 14: K2tog, K22, SSK. (24 sts)
Rnds 15–16: K all sts.
Rnd 17: K2tog, K20, SSK. (22 sts)
Rnd 18: K all sts.
Rnd 19: K2tog, K18, SSK. (20 sts)
Rnd 20: K all sts.
Rnd 21: K2tog, K16, SSK. (18 sts)
Rnd 22: K all sts.
Rnd 23: K2tog, K14, SSK. (16 sts)
Rnd 24: K all sts.

Rnd 23: K11, w&t, P4, w&t, K5, w&t, P6, w&t, K12.
Rnd 24: (K2tog, K1) 6 times. (12 sts)

Cut yarn, thread through remaining live sts, and pull closed. Use loose end to seam hole at bottom of paw closed.

Left Back Leg

Place 32 sts from scrap yarn onto 3 dpns. Rejoin color A at the next st in center of cat's belly, K32. Join sts in the round, K6 (new EOR). Repeat all rounds the same as the right leg.

Stuff your cat fully through the opening between back legs. Then hold sides of hole together and seam closed.

Ears (make 2 the same)

The ears are worked separately and seamed to head. Work begins at bottom of ear. CO 15 sts onto 3 dpns; join in the round.

Rnds 1–2: K all sts.
Rnd 3: K1, SSK, K2tog, K5, SSK, K2tog, K1. (11 sts)
Rnds 4–5: K all sts.
Rnd 6: SSK, K2tog, K3, SSK, K2tog. (7 sts)
Rnds 7–8: K all sts.

Cut yarn, thread through remaining live sts, pull closed. Flatten ears with the CO tail coming from one bottom corner. Bend slightly to create a slight hollowing in the front and seam to head at first decrease on each side, with about 5 sts between them.

All 4 of the Gentleman's Ginger's legs will need to be supported if you want it to stand up. Insert an extra dpn, chopstick, or other straight, thin stick up through the bottom of the paw and into the body as far as it will go. Leave 1–2 in./2.5–5 cm at the bottom to stick into a block of Styrofoam.

Rnd 25: K2tog, K12, SSK. (14 sts)
Rnd 26: K all sts.
Rnd 27: K2tog, K10, SSK. (12 sts)
Rnd 28: K all sts.
Row 29: K10, turn work.
Row 30: Slip 1, P7, turn work.
Row 31: Slip 1, K7.

Arrange these 8 sts on 2 dpns, and with RS facing work a 3-needle bind-off. Cut yarn and pull through last st. Turn work RS out again.

Sts are now picked up on each side of the bind-off seam to work the lower part of the leg. With RS facing, begin at the bind-off seam and pick up/knit the following sts with 3 dpns:

1st dpn: PU 4 sts from bind-off seam to live sts.
2nd dpn: K the 4 live sts.
3rd dpn: PU 4 sts from live sts to bind-off seam (EOR). (12 sts)

Note: If working optional stripes with color C, use it for Rnds 3, 4, 9, and 10.

Rnds 1–20: K all sts.

Switch to color B to work the paw (optional).

Rnd 21: K3, (M1, K1) 6 times, K3. (18 sts)
Rnd 22: K all sts.

The nursery is where the Morgan children, especially the twins, spend a sizable portion of their day. Although they get new toys on Christmas and for their birthdays, the Morgan children are not spoiled, so when their mother told them they could keep a six-week-old litter of kittens in the nursery, they were delighted to have a new distraction and promised not to let them claw the rug. The kittens provide the twins with entertainment between lessons and moments of hysterical giggling throughout the day—quickly quelled by the governess. She wishes Mrs. Morgan had asked her for her opinion before allowing the kittens in.

Trudy has taught the black kitten to roll over, and Timmy can get the grey one to jump up onto the rocking horse. They're planning a "Kitten Circus" for the family this coming Saturday and have made tickets for everyone in the house to come and watch.

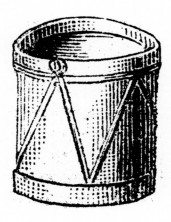

The Nursery Kittens

FINISHED SIZE
- 6 in./15 cm long (not including tail)
- 4 in./10 cm tall

YARN
Woolfolk Tage Yarn: 55 yd./50.5 m total per kitten
(color A: 40 yd./26.5 m; color B: 15 yd./13.5 m)
- Kitten 1: Color 05 (A: black); Color 00 (B: white)
- Kitten 2: Color 24 (A: gray); Color 00 (B: white)
- Kitten 3: Color 21 (A: light
  beige); Color 00 (B: white)

Note: Although this particular yarn is classified as
worsted weight on Ravelry, it is more like a fingering
or light DK weight when used to knit a stuffed
animal, which requires a tighter fabric. If looking for
a substitute yarn to use on this project, please keep
that point in mind.

NEEDLES
- US size 3/3.25 mm double-pointed needles

INSTRUCTIONS

Chest

Work begins at neckline. The chest is worked flat
with the intarsia method of colorwork. Two sections
of color A border a center section of color B.

Begin by preparing a second, small ball of color A
for the second side. When changing colors, bring

the new color over the old one to prevent a gap from
forming between them. CO the following colors and
number of sts onto 1 dpn:
- Color A: CO 6 sts
- Color B: CO 10 sts
- Color A: CO 6 sts

Row 1: Color A: P6; Color B: P10; Color A: P6.
Row 2: Color A: K6; Color B: K10; Color A: K6.
Row 3: Color A: P6; Color B: P10; Color A: P6.
Row 4: Color A: K7; Color B: K8; Color A: K7.
Row 5: Color A: P7; Color B: P8; Color A: P7.
Row 6: Color A: K7; Color B: K8; Color A: K7.
Row 7: Color A: P7; Color B: P8; Color A: P7.
Row 8: Color A: K8; Color B: K6; Color A: K8.
Row 9: Color A: P8; Color B: P6; Color A: P8.
Row 10: Color A: K8; Color B: K6; Color A: K8.
Row 11: Color A: P8; Color B: P6; Color A: P8.
Row 12: Color A: K9; Color B: K4; Color A: K9.
Row 13: Color A: P9; Color B: P4; Color A: P9.

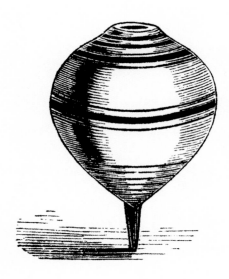

Slip the first 9 sts (first color A section) onto 1 dpn without knitting them. Rows 14–16 are worked on the center (color B) sts only.

Row 14: Color B: K4.
Row 15: Color B: P4.
Row 16: Color B: K4.

Slip all color B sts and the last section of color A sts onto a piece of scrap yarn.

Joints (all 4 legs)

All 4 of the kitten's legs include a joint, which is worked the same way in all of them. Refer to these instructions whenever knitting a joint is called for.

1. Slip 1, P7, turn work.
2. Slip 1, K7.
3. Arrange the 8 sts just worked onto 2 dpns, the remaining 2 sts on a third.
4. With RS together, work a 3-needle bind-off over the 8 sts.
5. Cut yarn and pull through last st.
6. Turn work RS out.

This will form a tiny cup-shaped structure. Sts are now picked up/knitted around the top edge of this to work the lower leg. Beginning at the bind-off seam, pick up/knit the following sts with 3 dpns:

1st dpn: PU 4 sts from bind-off seam to 2 live sts.
2nd dpn: K2 live sts.
3rd dpn: PU 4 sts from live sts to bind-off seam (EOR). (10 sts)

Paws (all 4)

All 4 of the kitten's paws are worked the same way. Refer to these instructions whenever knitting a paw is called for. Cut color A; join color B.

Rnd 1: K3, M1, K2, M1, K3. (10 sts)
Rnd 2: K all sts.
Rnd 3: K6, w&t, P2, w&t, K3, w&t, P4, w&t, K7.

Cut yarn and thread through live sts. Pull closed, using loose end to seam hole closed on bottom of paw.

Right Front Leg

The right leg is worked over the first section of color A sts.

Setup: K9, and then PU 1 st in center of color B edge. Arrange these 10 sts onto 3 dpns; join in the round.

Rnds 1–2: K all sts.
Row 3: K5, turn work.

Work joint (see page 113), and then proceed with lower leg.

Rnds 1–2: K all sts.
Rnd 3: K2tog, K6, SSK.
Rnds 4–11: K all sts.

Work paw (see page 113).

Left Front Leg

Setup: Place the remaining color A sts onto a dpn, leaving the 4 color B sts on scrap yarn. With WS facing, PUP 1 st in center of color B edge, turn work. K10. Arrange these 10 sts onto 3 dpns; join in the round.

Rnds 1–2: K all sts.
Row 3: K3, turn work.

Work joint, lower leg, and paw the same as the right leg.

Belly

The belly and the back are both worked flat and then seamed together on the sides. When casting on a new stitch to the working needle, use the backwards loop cast-on. Place the 4 live color B sts onto 1 dpn. With WS facing, rejoin color B at first st.

Row 1: P all sts.
Row 2: CO 1 to working needle, K4, CO 1 to EOR. (6 sts)
Row 3: P all sts.
Row 4: K all sts.
Row 5: P all sts.
Row 6: CO 1 to working needle, K6, CO 1 to EOR. (8 sts)
Rows 7–18: Work in stockinette stitch.

Cut color B yarn. Place live sts on a piece of scrap yarn or leave on dpn.

Back

Seam first and last original CO sts together to form a circle that will become the neck opening for working later. Sts are now picked up around the edge of the upper legs to work the back.

Beginning at the joint of the left leg (close to the color B stitches) with RS facing and color A yarn,

PU 12 sts along the edge between the joint and the top/center where sts were seamed together.

With a second dpn, PU 12 more sts from the top/center down to the joint on the right leg (EOR). (24 sts) Sts can be arranged all on 1 dpn after a few rows.

Rows 1–13: Beginning with a P row, work 13 rows of stockinette stitch.
Row 14: K10, SSK, K2tog, K10. (22 sts)
Row 15: P all sts.
Row 16: K all sts.
Row 17: P all sts.
Row 18: K9, SSK, K2tog, K9. (20 sts)
Row 19: P all sts.
Row 20: K all sts.
Row 21: P all sts.
Row 22: K all sts.

Place the belly sts on a dpn. Separate the back sts onto 2 dpns (if they were transferred all on one). Join sts in the round; color A is used for the remainder of the back.

Row 23: K8 color B sts, and then K10 color A sts (new EOR). (28 sts)
Row 24: K2, w&t, P4, w&t, K2.
Row 25: K3, w&t, P6, w&t, K3.
Row 26: K4, w&t, P8, w&t, K3, place last st in round plus first st in next round on a small piece of scrap yarn, CO 1 new st to EOR.
Row 27: CO 1 new st to working needle, K4, w&t, P10, w&t, K5.
Row 28: K6, w&t, P12, w&t, K6.

Right Back Leg

Setup: K14, place remaining 14 sts on scrap yarn. Arrange the first 14 on 3 dpns and join in the round. K11 (new EOR).

Rnd 1: K all sts.
Rnd 2: K2tog, K10, SSK. (12 sts)
Rnds 3–6: K all sts.
Rnd 7: K4, SSK, K2tog, K4. (10 sts)
Rnd 8: K9, turn work.

Work joint (page 113).

Rnd 1: K all sts.
Rnd 2: K2tog, K6, SSK. (8 sts)
Rnds 3–7: K all sts.

Work paw (page 113).

Left Back Leg

The left leg is worked a little differently so that it will point forward. Arrange 14 sts from scrap yarn onto 3 dpns. With WS facing, rejoin color A at first st on top of kitten (below opening for tail). Rows 1–4 are worked flat.

Row 1: P2, w&t, K2.
Row 2: P3, w&t, K3.
Row 3: P4, w&t, K4.
Row 4: P5, w&t, K5.
Rnd 5: Join sts in the round, K3 (new EOR).

Rnd 6: K all sts.
Rnd 7: K2tog, K10, SSK. (12 sts)
Rnds 8–9: K all sts.
Rnd 10: K4, SSK, K2tog, K4. (10 sts)
Rnd 11: K9, turn work.

Work joint, lower leg, and paw the same as the right back leg.

Seam belly to back on both sides with either color A or color B; leave hole between legs open for now.

Tail

Setup: Place 2 live sts from scrap yarn onto 1 dpn. Sts are now picked up around the opening beneath the live sts. With RS facing, begin at the bottom/center of the opening and pick up/knit the following sts with 3 dpns and color A:

1st dpn: PU 3 sts from bottom/center to live sts.
2nd dpn: K2.
3rd dpn: PU 3 sts from live sts to bottom/center. (8 sts)

Join sts in the round.

Rnds 1–4: K all sts.
Rnd 5: K2tog, K6. (7 sts)
Rnds 6–9: K all sts.
Rnd 10: K5, SSK. (6 sts)
Rnds 11–14: K all sts.
Rnd 15: K2tog, K4 all on 1 dpn. (5 sts)
Rows 16–19: Work 4 rows of a 5-st I-cord—without turning, slide the stitches to the other end of the needle and pull up the working yarn from the last stitch to start the next row.

Row 20: K2tog, K3 (pulling up yarn from last st). (4 sts)
Row 21: Work 1 row of a 4-st I-cord.

Cut yarn, thread through remaining live sts, and pull closed.

Head

Sts are now picked up in the neck opening to work the head with color A. Begin where the first and last CO sts were joined at the top/center of the neck. The 22 sts that are picked up in Rnds 1–8 are picked up directly in the original CO sts. Rows 1–7 are worked flat; turn work after each one.

Row 1: PU 2 sts. (2 sts)
Row 2: Slip 1, P1, PUP 2 (these 2 are on the other side of the center). (4 sts)
Row 3: Slip 1, K3, PU2. (6 sts)
Row 4: Slip 1, P5, PUP 2. (8 sts)
Row 5: Slip 1, K7, PU 2. (10 sts)
Row 6: Slip 1, P9, PUP 2. (12 sts)
Row 7: Slip 1, K5 (new EOR).
Rnd 8: K6, PU 10 in color B CO sts, K6. (22 sts)
Row 9: K2, (M1, K1) 4 times, w&t, P16, w&t, (K1, M1) 4 times, K2. (30 sts)
Rnd 10: K all sts.
Row 11: K6, (M1, K1) 6 times, w&t, P30, w&t, (K1, M1) 6 times, K6. (42 sts)
Rnd 12: K all sts.
Rnd 13: K5, SSK, K2tog, K10, SSK, K2tog, K10, SSK, K2tog, K5. (36 sts)
Rnd 14: K4, SSK, K2tog, K20, SSK, K2tog, K4. (32 sts)
Rnd 15: K3, SSK, K2tog, K18, SSK, K2tog, K3. (28 sts)
Rnd 16: K2, SSK, K2tog, K16, SSK, K2tog, K2. (24 sts)
Rnd 17: K1, SSK, K2tog, K14, SSK, K2tog, K1. (20 sts)
Rnd 18: SSK, K2tog, K12, SSK, K2tog. (16 sts)
Rnd 19: K all sts.
Rnd 20: (K2tog) 8 times. (8 sts)

Cut yarn, thread through remaining live sts, and pull closed.

If safety eyes are used, stuff head first so it's easier to see where to attach them. Insert posts from the front of the face just below the decreases on each side and about 4 sts apart in the center. The back of the safety eye is then attached to the post from the inside of the kitten via the opening between the legs.

Stuff the remainder of the kitten now. Do so very loosely in the body. Stuffing in the legs is limited to the paws and joints, with light stuffing in the upper legs and none in lower legs. Only the first 4–5 rnds of the tail are stuffed.

Ears (make 2 the same)

The ears are worked separately and seamed to head. CO 10 sts onto 3 dpns.

Rnds 1–2: K all sts.
Rnd 3: SSK, K2tog, K2, SSK, K2tog. (6 sts)
Rnds 4–5: K all sts.

Cut yarn, thread through remaining live sts, and pull closed. Flatten ear with the CO tail coming from one corner. Seam CO edge to top of head with the CO tail.

Finishing

Once the stuffing is done, the opening between the legs can now be seamed closed. To create the proper forward positioning of the left leg, hold the 2 sides together with left leg pointing toward the head and begin at the top of the opening, working downward.

Any of the 4 legs can be placed in a desired position and tacked to body with color A. Similarly, supports in the legs may be necessary for the kitten to stand.

Grandad is Mr. Morgan's father and Aunt Pru's brother. He was encouraged to come live with the family after his wife died three years ago. This encouragement came mostly from his daughter-in-law, who gets along very well with him and thought he might help to ease the tension between herself and Aunt Pru, which he has somewhat.

Mr. Morgan Senior was a university professor before retirement and walks a mile and a half each Wednesday afternoon to meet up with his old friends and colleagues at their favorite tavern. The walk home is always a mixture of warm feelings from the pub and apprehension of the look he knows he'll get from his sister. He sometimes waits on a bench outside the house until he's sure she is in her boudoir.

Grandad spends most evenings playing billiards with his silver tabby watching. The cat is allowed to lie on one side of the table, his fur smelling of pipe tobacco and whiskey, evidence of the elder's affection.

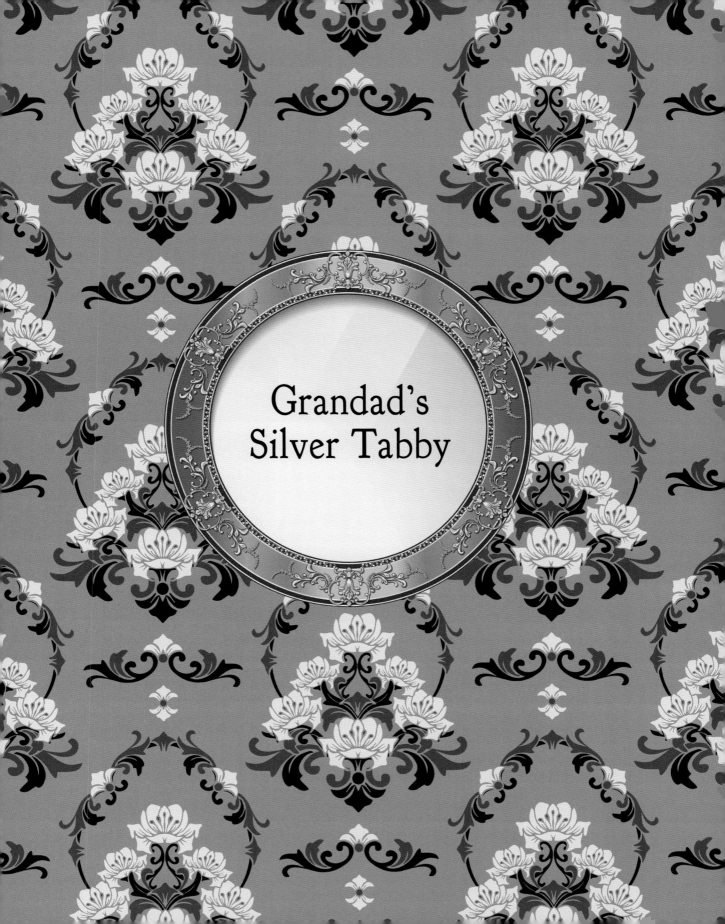

Grandad's Silver Tabby

FINISHED SIZE
- 16 in./40.5 cm long (not including tail)
- 6 in./15 cm wide

YARN
Juniper Moon Farm Herriot Great: 180 yd./164.5 m total (color A: 150 yd./137 m; color B: 30 yd./27.5 m)
- Cat 1: 101 Misty River (A);
  104 Charcoal Grey (B)
- Cat 2: 146 Fog (A); 104 Charcoal Grey (B)

NEEDLES
- US size 5/3.75 straight needles
- US size 5/3.75 mm double-pointed needles

NOTES
- Picking up and knitting the wraps is recommended after the color B short rows in the body since they are clearly visible. This is done on the first knit round immediately following each color B short row. The wraps from the color A short rows are less visible; therefore, picking up and knitting them is optional.
- Color changes: Rows worked with color B are noted in instructions. All others are worked with color A.

INSTRUCTIONS

Chest and Upper Legs
Work begins at neckline. CO 32 sts of color A onto 1 straight needle. Work 19 rows of straight stockinette stitch, beginning and ending with a P row.

Right Front Leg

Upper Leg
K16, place remaining sts on a piece of scrap yarn. Arrange the first 16 on 3 dpns; join in the round.

Rnd 1: K all sts.
Row 2: K5, turn work.
Row 3: Slip 1, P7, turn work.
Row 4: Slip 1, K7, turn work.
Row 5: Slip 1, P7.

Arrange these 8 sts on 2 dpns. With RS together work a 3-needle bind-off. Cut yarn. This creates the elbow. Turn work right-side out and, beginning at the bind-off seam, rejoin color A and PU/knit the following 18 sts with 3 dpns.

1st dpn: PU 5 sts from bind-off seam to live sts.

2nd dpn: K the 8 live sts.

3rd dpn: PU 5 sts from live sts to bind-off seam (EOR).

Join sts in the round to work the lower leg.

Lower Leg

Rnds 1–2: K all sts.

Rnd 3: K2tog, K14, SSK. (16 sts)

Rnds 4–5 (Color B): K all sts.

Rnd 6: K2tog, K12, SSK. (14 sts)

Rnds 7–8: K all sts.

Rnd 9: K2tog, K10, SSK. (12 sts)

Rnds 10–11: K all sts.

Rnd 12 (Color B): K2tog, K8, SSK. (10 sts)

Rnd 13 (Color B): K all sts.

Rnds 14–24: K all sts.

Rnd 25: K2, (M1, K2) 4 times. (14 sts)

Rnds 26–27: K all sts.

Rnd 28: K9, w&t, P4, w&t, K5, w&t, P6, w&t, K10 (EOR).

Cut yarn, thread through live sts, and pull closed. Use loose end to seam hole at bottom.

Left Front Leg

Place 16 sts from scrap yarn onto a dpn. With RS facing, rejoin color A at first st, K16. Arrange sts on 3 dpns and join in the round. All parts of the left leg and paw are worked exactly as the right leg except Row 2 of the upper leg, which is K3, turn work.

Body

When casting on new stitches to the working needle, use the backwards loop cast-on.

Setup: Pick up 54 sts between the front legs and along the two sides of the chest to begin the body. With the inside of the work facing (at first) and with color A, begin in the center between the front legs. It's best to use 4 dpns for this section; sts can be rearranged on the dpns later. The RS of work will be facing on dpns 2 and 3.

1st dpn: PU 6 sts from center of front legs to elbow of left leg.

2nd dpn: PU 16 sts from elbow of left leg along edge to top of chest, and then CO 5 sts.

3rd dpn: CO 5 new sts, and then PU 16 sts from top of right edge to elbow of right leg.

4th dpn: PU 6 sts from elbow of right leg to center of front legs (EOR).

Short rows are now worked along the bottom of the cat. All rows in the following section begin and end at the EOR between front legs.

Row 1: K4, w&t, P8, w&t, K4.
Row 2: K6, w&t, P12, w&t, K6.
Row 3: K8, w&t, P16, w&t, K8.
Row 4: K10, w&t, P20, w&t, K10, and then K42 (new EOR).

This new EOR will be here for the remainder of the body. Sts can be rearranged on the needles with a break here to designate it, or a stitch marker can be used. Work begins with another set of short rows to bend the body forward. All rows will begin and end at the EOR. The first row that is knit in the round is Rnd 6.

Row 1: K3, w&t, P6, w&t, K3.
Row 2: K6, w&t, P12, w&t, K6.

Row 3: K9, w&t, P18, w&t, K9.
Row 4: K12, w&t, P24, w&t, K12.
Row 5: K15, w&t, P30, w&t, K15.
Rnds 6–11: K all sts.

The next 6 rows/rounds are repeated 8 times on the body, with increases on the last 4 repeats to watch out for.

1. **Row 1 (Color B):** K24, w&t, P48, w&t, K24.
   Rnds 2–3: K all sts.
   Row 4: K14, w&t, P28, w&t, K14.
   Rnds 5–6: K all sts.
2. **Row 1 (Color B):** K24, w&t, P48, w&t, K24.
   Rnds 2–3: K all sts.
   Row 4: K14, w&t, P28, w&t, K14.
   Rnds 5–6: K all sts.
3. **Row 1 (Color B):** K24, w&t, P48, w&t, K24.
   Rnds 2–3: K all sts.
   Row 4: K14, w&t, P28, w&t, K14.
   Rnds 5–6: K all sts.
4. **Row 1 (Color B):** K24, w&t, P48, w&t, K24.
   Rnds 2–3: K all sts.
   Row 4: K14, w&t, P28, w&t, K14.
   Rnds 5–6: K all sts.
5. **Row 1 (Color B):** K24, w&t, P48, w&t, K24.
   Rnds 2–3: K all sts.
   Row 4: K14, w&t, P28, w&t, K14.
   Rnd 5: K all sts.
   Rnd 6: K1, M1R, K52, M1L, K1. (56 sts)

6. **Row 1 (Color B):** K25, w&t, P50, w&t, K25.
   Rnds 2–3: K all sts.
   Row 4: K14, w&t, P28, w&t, K14.
   Rnd 5: K all sts.
   Rnd 6: K1, M1R, K54, M1L, K1. (58 sts)
7. **Row 1 (Color B):** K26, w&t, P52, w&t, K26.
   Rnds 2–3: K all sts.
   Row 4: K14, w&t, P28, w&t, K14.
   Rnd 5: K all sts.
   Rnd 6: K1, M1R, K56, M1L, K1. (60 sts)
8. **Row 1 (Color B):** K27, w&t, P54, w&t, K27.
   Rnds 2–3: K all sts.
   Row 4: K14, w&t, P28, w&t, K14.
   Rnds 5–6: K all sts.

The following short rows will shape the end of the body. Row 7 creates an opening for the tail.

Row 1 (Color B): K4, w&t, P8, w&t, K4.
Row 2: K6, w&t, P12, w&t, K6.
Row 3: K8, w&t, P16, w&t, K8.
Row 4: K10, w&t, P20, w&t, K10.
Row 5 (Color B): K12, w&t, P24, w&t, K12.
Row 6: K14, w&t, P28, w&t, K14.

Row 7: K16, w&t, P32, w&t, K14, place last 2 sts in round, plus first 2 sts of next round onto a piece of scrap yarn, CO 2 new sts to EOR.
Row 8: CO 2 new sts to working needle, K16, w&t, P36, w&t, K18.
Row 9: K20, w&t, P40, w&t, K20.

Cut yarn. Place all live sts onto a piece of scrap yarn for working after the head and tail.

Head

Setup: Sts are now picked up around the top of the chest and across the back to work the head. With color A and RS facing, PU the first 10 sts from the sts that were cast-on behind the neck, and then PU 34 more for a total of 44 sts (EOR). Join in the round.

Rnd 1: K19, SSK, K2, K2tog, K19. (42 sts)
Rnd 2: K4, (M1, K2) 4 times, K18, (K2, M1) 4 times, K4. (50 sts)
Rnd 3: K22, SSK, K2, K2tog, K22. (48 sts)

The next section contains short rows to change the direction of the stitches. Each one begins and ends at the EOR. Knitting in the round resumes in Rnd 11.

Row 4: K3, w&t, P6, w&t, K3.
Row 5: K6, w&t, P12, w&t, K6.
Row 6: K9, w&t, P18, w&t, K9.
Row 7: K12, w&t, P24, w&t, K12.
Row 8: K15, w&t, P30, w&t, K15.
Row 9: K18, w&t, P36, w&t, K18.
Row 10: K21, w&t, P42, w&t, K21.
Rnd 11: K5, SSK, K2tog, K30, SSK, K2tog, K5. (44 sts)
Rnd 12: K19, SSK, K2, K2tog, K19. (42 sts)
Rnd 13: K4, SSK, K2tog, K26, SSK, K2tog, K4. (38 sts)
Rnd 14: K16, SSK, K2, K2tog, K16. (36 sts)
Rnd 15: K3, SSK, K2tog, K22, SSK, K2tog, K3. (32 sts)
Rnd 16: K all sts.
Rnd 17: K2, SSK, K2tog, K20, SSK, K2tog, K2. (28 sts)
Rnd 18: K all sts.
Rnd 19: K1, SSK, K2tog, K18, SSK, K2tog, K1. (24 sts)
Rnd 20: K all sts.
Rnd 21: (K2tog) 12 times. (12 sts)

Cut yarn, thread through remaining live sts, and pull closed.

Tail

Setup: Place 4 sts from scrap yarn onto 1 dpn. Sts are now picked up around the opening below the live sts to work the tail. With RS facing, begin at bottom/center of opening and PU/knit the following 14 sts with 3 dpns:

1st dpn: PU 5 sts from bottom/center up to live sts.
2nd dpn: K4 live sts.
3rd dpn: PU 5 sts from live sts down to bottom/center EOR, join in the round.

Rnds 1–6: K all sts.
Rnds 7–8 (Color B): K all sts; cut color B.

Repeat Rnds 1–8 six more times for a total of 7 color B stripes, and then continue below.

Rnds 9–10: K all sts.
Rnd 11: (K2tog, K5) 2 times. (12 sts)

Rnd 12: K all sts.
Rnd 13: (K2tog, K4) 2 times. (10 sts)
Rnd 14: K all sts.

Cut yarn, thread through remaining live sts, and pull closed.

Stuff front legs, chest, head, and tail now. Leave body unstuffed while working the back legs.

Right Back Leg

Setup: Place first 30 sts from scrap yarn onto 3 dpns; leave remaining 30 sts on scrap yarn. With RS facing, rejoin color A at first stitch, K30. CO 6 new sts to the end; join in the round. K7, new EOR. (36 sts)

Rnd 1: K all sts.
Rnds 2–3 (Color B): K all sts.
Rnd 4: K1, K2tog, K30, SSK, K1. (34 sts)
Rnd 5: K all sts.
Rnd 6: K1, K2tog, K28, SSK, K1. (32 sts)
Rnd 7: K all sts.
Rnd 8: K1, K2tog, K26, SSK, K1. (30 sts)
Rnd 9: K all sts.
Rnd 10 (Color B): K1, K2tog, K24, SSK, K1. (28 sts)
Rnd 11 (Color B): K all sts.
Rnd 12: K1, K2tog, K22, SSK, K1. (26 sts)
Rnd 13: K all sts.
Rnd 14: K1, K2tog, K20, SSK, K1. (24 sts)
Rnd 15: K all sts.
Rnd 16: K1, K2tog, K18, SSK, K1. (22 sts)
Rnd 17: K all sts.

Rnd 18 (Color B): K1, K2tog, K16, SSK, K1. (20 sts)

Rnd 19 (Color B): K all sts; cut color B.

Rnd 20: K1, K2tog, K14, SSK, K1. (18 sts)

Rnd 21: K all sts.

Rnd 22: K1, K2tog, K12, SSK, K1. (16 sts)

Rnd 23: K all sts.

Rnd 24: K1, K2tog, K10, SSK, K1. (14 sts)

Rnd 25: K all sts.

Row 26: K4, turn work.

Row 27: Slip 1, P7, turn work.

Row 28: Slip 1, K7, turn work.

Row 29: Slip 1, P7.

Arrange these 8 sts on 2 dpns. With RS together work a 3-needle bind-off. Cut yarn. This creates the elbow. Turn work RS out and, beginning at the bind-off seam, PU/knit the following 16 sts with 3 dpns:

1st dpn: PU 5 sts from bind-off seam to live sts.

2nd dpn: K the 6 live sts.

3rd dpn: PU 5 sts from live sts to bind-off seam (EOR).

Join sts in the round to work the bottom of the leg.

Rnd 1: K all sts.

Rnd 2: K2tog, K12, SSK. (14 sts)

Rnd 3: K all sts.

Rnd 4 (Color B): K2tog, K10, SSK. (12 sts)

Rnd 5 (Color B): K all sts.

Rnd 6: K2tog, K8, SSK. (10 sts)

Rnds 7–11: K all sts.

Rnds 12–13 (Color B): K all sts; cut color B.

Rnds 14–17: K all sts.

Rnd 18: K2, (M1, K2) 4 times. (14 sts)

Rnds 19–20: K all sts.

Rnd 21: K9, w&t, P4, w&t, K5, w&t, P6, w&t, K10.

Cut yarn, thread through live sts, and pull closed. Use loose end to seam hole at bottom of paw closed.

Left Back Leg

Place the remaining 30 sts from scrap yarn onto 3 dpns. With RS facing, rejoin color A at first st, K30. CO 6 new sts to the end; join in the round. K23, new EOR. (36 sts)

Work all rounds the same as the right leg from this point on.

Finish stuffing the body and both back legs now through opening between the back legs, and then seam the opening closed. If desired, hold back legs at different angles and seam in place.

When stuffing, keep in mind the curve in the cat's back. Also, the upper back leg should be more flat than round.

Ears (make 2 the same)

The ears are worked separately and seamed to head. Work begins at bottom of ear. With color A, CO 15 sts onto 3 dpns; join in the round.

Rnds 1–2: K all sts.

Rnd 3: K1, SSK, K2tog, K5, SSK, K2tog, K1. (11 sts)

Rnds 4–5: K all sts.

Rnd 6: SSK, K2tog, K3, SSK, K2tog. (7 sts)

Rnds 7–8: K all sts.

Cut yarn, thread through remaining live sts, pull closed. Flatten ears with the CO tail coming from one bottom corner. Bend slightly to create a slight hollowing in the front, and seam to head at the first decrease on each side.

The scullery in Victorian times was a room off the kitchen where the dirtiest and most physical work took place. Pans were scoured, laundry was scrubbed, and chamber pots were emptied. The scullery maid in this house might have felt very isolated if not for the company of a friendly cat who didn't seem to mind where he spent his day.

Despite the dirtiness around him, this cat takes pride in his appearance and spends most of the day licking his paw and running it over his neck and head. Water splashed on him from a sink full of dishes or a soapy mop bucket doesn't dissuade him from wanting to live in the scullery, and dirty plates sometimes have bits of meat left on them, don't they?

The Scullery Cat

FINISHED SIZE

- 14 in./35.5 cm tall
- 6 in./15 cm wide
- 12 in./30.5 cm deep (not including tail)

YARN

Yarn Bee Tender Touch: 200 yd./183 m total (color A: 180 yd./164.5 m; color B/optional: 20 yd./18.5 m)

- Cat 1: 101 Rain
- Cat 2: 102 Dove (A); 100 Snow (B)

Needles

- US size 4/3.5 mm straight needles
- US size 4/3.5 mm double-pointed needles

INSTRUCTIONS

Chest

Work begins at neckline and is worked flat with the intarsia method of colorwork. When switching colors, always remember to bring the new color over the old one to prevent a gap from forming between them.

Begin by preparing a second ball of color A (about 20 armlengths), so that you'll have one ball for each side of the needle with color B sts in the center. CO the following colors and number of sts onto one straight needle:

- Color A: CO 9 sts
- Color B: CO 22 sts
- Color A: CO 9 sts (40 sts)

Row 1: Color A: P9; Color B: P22; Color A: P9.
Row 2: Color A: SSK, K8; Color B: K20; Color A: K8, K2tog. (38 sts)

Row 3: Color A: P9; Color B: P20; Color A: P9.
Row 4: Color A: SSK, K8; Color B: K18; Color A: K8, K2tog. (36 sts)
Row 5: Color A: P9; Color B: P18; Color A: P9.
Row 6: Color A: SSK, K8; Color B: K16; Color A: K8, K2tog. (34 sts)
Row 7: Color A: P9; Color B: P16; Color A: P9.
Row 8: Color A: SSK, K8; Color B: K14; Color A: K8, K2tog. (32 sts)
Row 9: Color A: P9; Color B: P14; Color A: P9.
Row 10: Color A: K10; Color B: K12; Color A: K10.
Row 11: Color A: P10; Color B: P12; Color A: P10.
Row 12: Color A: K11; Color B: K10; Color A: K11.
Row 13: Color A: P11; Color B: P10; Color A: P11.
Row 14: Color A: K12; Color B: K8; Color A: K12.
Row 15: Color A: P12; Color B: P8; Color A: P12.
Row 16: Color A: K13; Color B: K6; Color A: K13.
Row 17: Color A: P13; Color B: P6; Color A: P13.
Row 18: Color A: K14; Color B: K4; Color A: K14.
Row 19: Color A: P14; Color B: P4; Color A: P14.

Row 20: Color A: K15; Color B: K2; Color A: K15.
Row 21: Color A: P15; Color B: P2; Color A: P15.

Cut color B and second ball of color A. The last 3 rows of the chest are worked with the first ball of color A only.

Rows 22–24: K all sts.

Front Left Leg (straight)

Slip last 16 sts of Row 24 onto 3 dpns without knitting them. Place remaining 16 sts onto a piece of scrap yarn. Join sts in the round for the rounds below. The increases in Rnd 37 will shape the toes on the front of the paw.

Rnds 1–6: K all sts.
Rnd 7: K2tog, K12, SSK. (14 sts)
Rnds 8–12: K all sts.
Rnd 13: K2tog, K10, SSK. (12 sts)
Rnds 14–35: K all sts.
Rnd 36: K2tog, K8, SSK. (10 sts)
Rnd 37: K3, (Kfbf) 4 times, K3. (18 sts)
Rnds 38–41: K all sts.

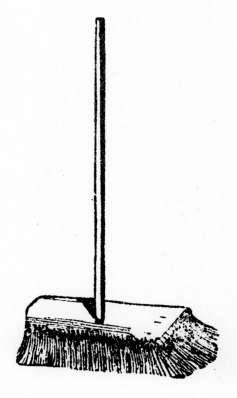

Cut yarn, thread through remaining live sts, and pull closed. Stitch hole at bottom of paw closed with the loose end.

Front Right Leg (bent)

Place 16 sts from scrap yarn onto 1 dpn. Rejoin working yarn, and with RS facing, K10. On your working needle, pull the second st from end over the first one and off the needle (bind off 1 st). K1, pull off second st again. Repeat 5 more times for a total of 7 bind-off sts; 9 live sts remain on the working needle—8 together and 1 on the tip, separated by a gap of the 7 bind-off stitches. There are none on the left needle at that point.

Slide the single st next to the first st on same dpn (thus joining the sts in the round). Now slip the second st (formerly the first one) over the first one and off the needle; 8 sts remain. Work the rows below back and forth with 2 dpns:

Row 1: Slip 1, K7.
Row 2: Slip 1, P7.

Repeat these 2 rows twice for a total of 6 rows worked in stockinette stitch. Arrange 8 sts onto 2 dpns with RS together; work a 3-needle bind-off. Cut yarn, thread through last st, and pull closed. Turn work RS out.

Sts are now picked up around the elbow to shape the leg. Rejoin working yarn, and with RS facing and bind-off sts pointing downward, pick up the following sts with 3 dpns:

1st dpn: PU 6 sts in the bind-off sts at elbow crease.
2nd dpn: PU 5 sts along one edge of elbow.
3rd dpn: PU 5 sts along other edge of elbow. (16 sts)

First st in round will be the first st picked up in elbow crease.

Rnds 1–2: K all sts.
Rnd 3: K1, SSK, K2tog, K11. (14 sts)
Rnds 4–5: K all sts.
Rnd 6: SSK, K2tog, K10. (12 sts)
Rnds 7–28: K all sts.
Rnd 29: K2tog, K8, SSK. (10 sts)

Rnds 30–31: K all sts.
Rnd 32: K3, M1, K4, M1, K3. (12 sts)
Rnd 33: K all sts.
Rnd 34: K2, w&t, P4, w&t, K2.
Rnd 35: K3, w&t, P6, w&t, K3.
Rnd 36: K4, w&t, P8, w&t, K4.
Rnd 37: K all sts.

Cut yarn, thread through remaining live sts, and pull closed. Use loose end to stitch hole closed.

Back

Seam top 4 rows of chest together, forming a circle to shape the neck. Rejoin working yarn, and with RS facing, PU the following sts to begin the back:

1st dpn: PU 19 sts from neck to elbow.
2nd dpn: PU 6 sts from elbow to seam of left leg.
3rd dpn: PU 19 sts from seam of left leg to neck.
  (44 sts)

Sts can be rearranged on your dpns to make them easier to work with.

Row 1: K4, w&t, P8, w&t, K4.
Row 2: K6, w&t, P12, w&t, K6.

Row 3: K8, w&t, P16, w&t, K8.
Row 4: K10, w&t, P20, w&t, K10.

Rnds 5–11 are worked in the round over all the sts:

Rnd 5: K all sts.
Rnd 6: K2, (M1, K4) 4 times, M1, K8, (M1, K4) 4 times, M1, K2. (54 sts)
Rnds 7–8: K all sts.
Rnd 9: K2, (M1, K5) 4 times, M1, K10, (M1, K5) 4 times, M1, K2. (64 sts)
Rnds 10–11: K all sts.

Short rows are again worked on just some of the sts.

Row 12: K8, w&t, P16, w&t, K8.
Row 13: K9, w&t, P18, w&t, K9.
Row 14: K10, w&t, P20, w&t, K10.
Row 15: K11, w&t, P22, w&t, K11.
Row 16: K12, w&t, P24, w&t, K12.
Row 17: K13, w&t, P26, w&t, K13.
Row 18: K14, w&t, P28, w&t, K14.
Row 19: K15, w&t, P30, w&t, K15.
Row 20: K16, w&t, P32, w&t, K16.
Row 21: K17, w&t, P34, w&t, K17.
Row 22: K18, w&t, P36, w&t, K18.
Row 23: K19, w&t, P38, w&t, K19.
Row 24: K20, w&t, P40, w&t, K20.

The remainder of the back is worked in the round over all of the sts.

Rnd 25: K all sts.
Rnd 26: K30, K2tog, SSK, K30. (62 sts)
Rnds 27–28: K all sts.
Rnd 29: K29, K2tog, SSK, K29. (60 sts)
Rnds 30–31: K all sts.
Rnd 32: K28, K2tog, SSK, K28. (58 sts)
Rnds 33–34: K all sts.
Rnd 35: K27, K2tog, SSK, K27. (56 sts)
Rnds 36–37: K all sts.
Rnd 38: K26, K2tog, SSK, K26. (54 sts)
Rnds 39–40: K all sts.
Rnd 41: K25, K2tog, SSK, K25. (52 sts)
Rnds 42–43: K all sts.
Rnd 44: K24, K2tog, SSK, K24. (50 sts)
Rnds 45–50: K all sts.

Tail

Setup rnd:

1st dpn: K6, place next 38 sts on scrap yarn.
2nd dpn: CO 3 new sts, place a marker, CO 3 new sts.
3rd dpn: K remaining 6 live sts. (18 sts)

Join sts in the round and knit remaining 6 sts plus 9 more. You are now at the marker (EOR).

Rnds 1–3: K all sts.
Rnd 4: K2tog, K14, SSK. (16 sts)
Rnds 5–9: K all sts.
Rnd 10: K2tog, K12, SSK. (14 sts)
Rnds 11–15: K all sts.
Rnd 16: K2tog, K10, SSK. (12 sts)

Knit all sts for 60 rounds. Then work end of tail:

Rnd 1: K2tog, K8, SSK. (10 sts)
Rnds 2–3: K all sts.
Rnd 4: K2tog, K6, SSK. (8 sts)
Rnd 5: K all sts.

Cut yarn, thread through remaining live sts, and pull closed.

Head

Sts are now picked up in the original CO sts to work the neck and head. With back of cat facing, count 9 sts to the right of the first CO st (center/back of neck). Beginning with the 9th st and working to the left, PU 5 sts (about 1 in every other CO st) until you are back at the center. Place a stitch marker, and then, beginning with the next st, PU 5 more sts on the other side of the center st (about 1 in every other CO st again) for a total of 10 sts across the back of your cat's neck. Work the following rows back and forth with 2 dpns:

Row 1: P all sts.
Row 2: K all sts.
Row 3: P all sts.
Row 4: K all sts.

With a second dpn and beginning where you left off on the left side, PU 11 sts between there and the front/center of your cat's chest (1 st in every CO st). With a third dpn, PU 11 sts from the front/center st to the sts in the back on the other side. (32 sts)

Join sts in the round and K5 to reach the marker. There will be small gaps on either side of the back sts—these will not be visible once you get going. Begin with the following short rows back and forth:

Row 1: K5, w&t, P10, w&t, K5.
Row 2: K6, w&t, P12, w&t, K6.
Row 3: K7, w&t, P14, w&t, K7.
Row 4: K8, w&t, P16, w&t, K8.
Row 5: K9, w&t, P18, w&t, K9.
Row 6: K10, w&t, P20, w&t, K10.

The rest of the head is worked over all of the sts.

Rnd 7: K3, (M1, K3) 3 times, K2, K2tog, SSK, K2, (K3, M1) 3 times, K3. (36 sts)
Rnd 8: K all sts.
Rnd 9: K1, (M1, K2) 6 times, K3, K2tog, SSK, K3, (K2, M1) 6 times, K1. (46 sts)
Rnd 10: K all sts.
Rnd 11: K21, K2tog, SSK, K21. (44 sts)
Rnd 12: K all sts.
Rnd 13: K3, place next 4 sts on scrap yarn, CO 4 new sts, K13, K2tog, SSK, K13, place next 4 sts on scrap yarn, CO 4 new sts, K3. (42 sts)
Rnd 14: (M1, K1) 3 times, K36, (M1, K1) 3 times. (48 sts)
Rnd 15: K all sts.

Rnd 16: K4, SSK, K2tog, K32, SSK, K2tog, K4. (44 sts)
Rnd 17: K all sts.
Rnd 18: K3, SSK, K2tog, K30, SSK, K2tog, K3. (40 sts)
Rnd 19: K all sts.
Rnd 20: K2, SSK, K2tog, K6, SSK, K2tog, K8, SSK, K2tog, K6, SSK, K2tog, K2. (32 sts)
Rnd 21: K all sts.
Rnd 22: K1, SSK, K2tog, K4, SSK, K2tog, K6, SSK, K2tog, K4, SSK, K2tog, K1. (24 sts)
Rnd 23: K all sts.
Rnd 24: SSK, K2tog, K2, SSK, K2tog, K4, SSK, K2tog, K2, SSK, K2tog. (16 sts)
Rnd 25: K all sts.
Rnd 26: K2tog, K1, SSK, K2tog, K2, SSK, K2tog, K1, SSK. (10 sts)
Rnd 27: K all sts; remove stitch marker.
Row 28: K2, turn work, slip 1, P3, turn work, slip 1, K3, turn work, slip 1, P3, turn work, SSK, K2tog.

Cut yarn, leaving a tail of 6–7 in./15–18 cm. Thread through 6 live sts at bottom, followed by top 2 sts. Pull closed but don't trim. Proceed to ears before stuffing.

The loose end serves both to bring up the right paw to your cat's mouth and direct the head downward. After stuffing your cat in entirety, thread the end into a darning needle, insert into the "wrist" and pull to tighten. Repeat this step 2–3 times; secure end.

Left Ear

Place 4 sts from scrap yarn onto 1 dpn. Rejoin working yarn, and with RS facing and 2 additional dpns, PU 10 sts around opening (5 sts on each). Join sts in the round and work the rounds below. The first st of the round will be the first one from scrap yarn toward center of head.

Rnds 1–3: K all sts. (14 sts)
Rnd 4: K8, SSK, K2tog, K2. (12 sts)
Rnd 5: K all sts.
Rnd 6: K7, SSK, K2tog, K1. (10 sts)
Rnd 7: K all sts.
Rnd 8: K6, SSK, K2tog. (8 sts)

Cut yarn, thread through remaining live sts, and pull closed.

Right Ear

Setup and finishing is the same as for the left ear. The first st of the round is the first one held on scrap yarn away from center of head.

Rnds 1–3: K all sts. (14 sts)
Rnd 4: K7, SSK, K2tog, K3. (12 sts)
Rnd 5: K all sts.
Rnd 6: K6, SSK, K2tog, K2. (10 sts)
Rnd 7: K all sts.
Rnd 8: K5, SSK, K2tog, K1. (8 sts)

Stuff tail, front legs, head, and about half of the body now.

Base

Place 38 sts from scrap yarn onto 2 dpns. PU 12 sts on edge of tail; join in the round. First st in round is the first one from scrap yarn. Sts may be rearranged on your dpns as needed:

Rnd 1: K all sts. (50 sts)
Rnd 2: (K2tog, K3) 10 times. (40 sts)
Rnd 3: K all sts.
Rnd 4: (K2tog, K2) 10 times. (30 sts)
Rnd 5: K all sts.
Rnd 6: (K2tog, K1) 10 times. (20 sts)
Rnd 7: K all sts.

Complete stuffing, and then finish closing the base with the rounds below:

Rnd 8: (K2tog) 10 times. (10 sts)
Rnd 9: K all sts.

Cut yarn, thread through remaining live sts, and pull closed.

Back Legs (make 2)

Back legs are worked separately and seamed to bottom of cat. CO 12 sts onto 3 dpns, leaving a tail of 5–6 in./12.5–15 cm; join sts in the round.

Rnds 1–4: K all sts.
Rnd 5: K4, SSK, K2tog, K4. (10 sts)
Rnds 6–7: K all sts.
Rnd 8: K3, M1, K4, M1, K3. (12 sts)
Rnd 9: K all sts.
Rnd 10: K2, w&t, P4, w&t, K2.
Rnd 11: K3, w&t, P6, w&t, K3.
Rnd 12: K4, w&t, P8, w&t, K4.
Rnd 13: K all sts.

Cut yarn, thread through remaining live sts, and pull closed. Use the loose end to stitch hole at bottom of paw closed. Stuff loosely; seam about half of it to the bottom of your cat.

The children's dollhouse, like the Morgans' full-sized house, has many windows for cats to sit in. Mrs. Morgan designed a tiny knitted cat in the same position as the cat that sits in their windows. Although larger than the 1:12 ratio of their home's furnishings, the doll family appreciates her efforts and welcomes the cats as beloved family pets.

Tiny
Window
Cat

FINISHED SIZE
- 3 in./7.5 cm tall
- 2 in./5 cm wide (not including tail)

YARN
Gedifra Laura: 20 yd./18.5 m total
- Gray cat: Color 3206
- Orange cat: Color 3214
- Black cat: Color 3207

Note: Although this particular yarn is classified as Aran weight on Ravelry, it is barely fingering weight when knitted for a stuffed animal. If looking for a substitute yarn to use on this project, please keep that point in mind.

NEEDLES
- US size 1/2.25 mm double-pointed needles

INSTRUCTIONS

Body, Neck, and Head
Work begins at the bottom of cat. CO 28 sts onto 3 dpns and join in the round.

Rnds 1–14: K all sts.
Rnd 15: (K2tog) 2 times, K20, (SSK) 2 times. (24 sts)
Rnd 16: K all sts.
Rnd 17: (K2tog) 2 times, K16, (SSK) 2 times. (20 sts)
Rnd 18: K all sts.
Rnd 19: (K2tog) 2 times, K12, (SSK) 2 times. (16 sts)
Rnd 20: K all sts.
Rnd 21: K2tog, K12, SSK. (14 sts)
Rnd 22: K all sts.
Rnd 23: K5, SSK, K2tog, K5. (12 sts)
Rnd 24: (M1R, K5, M1L, K1) 2 times. (16 sts)
Rnd 25: K all sts.

Rnd 26: (M1R, K7, M1L, K1) 2 times. (20 sts)
Rnds 27–28: K all sts.
Rnd 29: (K2tog, K5, SSK, K1) 2 times. (16 sts)
Rnd 30: K all sts.

Ears

Slip the first 3 sts in the round onto a dpn without knitting them. Slip next 10 sts onto a piece of scrap yarn. Arrange the 6 active sts onto 3 dpns and join them in the round.

Rnds 1–2: K all sts.
Rnd 3: (K2tog) 3 times. (3 sts)

Cut yarn, leaving a tail of 10–12 in./25.5–30.5 cm. Thread through remaining 3 sts and pull closed. Weave the loose end down the inside of the ear, and then slip the first 2 sts from the scrap yarn onto the working yarn. The working yarn is now in position to work the second ear.

Arrange the next 6 sts from scrap yarn onto 3 dpns, leaving the last 2 sts on the scrap yarn. Join in the round and repeat Rnds 1–3 above. Weave the loose end down inside of ear, and then thread through the last 2 sts from scrap yarn. Pull to cinch all 4 sts together, closing top of head. Weave in loose ends, seaming small holes on inside of ears closed.

Stuff cat's head and body; ears are not stuffed.

Base

Sts are now picked up in the original CO sts to work the base. With RS facing, begin in the first CO st and PU 28 sts with 3 dpns; join in the round.

Rnd 1: K all sts.
Rnd 2: (K2tog, K2) 7 times. (21 sts)
Rnd 3: K all sts.
Rnd 4: (K2tog, K1) 7 times. (14 sts)
Rnd 5: K all sts.
Rnd 6: (K2tog) 7 times. (7 sts)

Cut yarn, leaving a tail of 6–8 in./15–20.5 cm. Thread through remaining live sts and pull closed. Flatten the base, and then pinch together the top edge of it with your fingers. Use the tail to help define and shape it by making a whipstitch all around the edge.

Tail

CO 6 sts onto 1 dpn and work 30 rows of a 6-st I-cord—without turning, slide the stitches to the other end of the needle and pull up the working yarn from the last stitch to start the next row. Then (K2tog) 3 times, cut yarn, and pull through remaining live sts. Seam to bottom of cat on side with the body decreases.

There are several fireplaces in the Morgan family home. Their crackling sounds create a comforting background noise, which the family isn't even aware of but would miss if it suddenly stopped—a reassuring beat from the heart of the home.

One cat in particular is attached to these fireplaces. She is thought to be the oldest cat in the house and has Mr. and Mrs. Morgan's permission to sleep in front of whichever of them she chooses on any day. Household members have strict instructions that she is not to be disturbed.

This cat originally belonged to the family that lived in the house before the Morgans, and they said she was eighteen years old at that time—which would make her thirty-five now. Of course, that could be just a story told by Grandad, tinderbox in hand, around the same fireplace where this old cat sleeps.

The Fireplace Cat

FINISHED SIZE

- 11 in./28 cm side to side
- 10 in./25.5 cm front to back
- 5 in./12.5 cm top to bottom

YARN

Cascade Aereo: 200 yd./183 m total
- Dark gray cat: 02 Charcoal
- Light gray cat: 03 Silver
- Light tan cat: 05 Doeskin Heather

NEEDLES

- US size 5/3.75 mm double-pointed needles

INSTRUCTIONS

Body

Work begins at the bottom/center of neckline. CO 48 sts onto 3 dpns; join in the round. A 5th dpn (or circular needle) will be needed once sts are increased beyond what 3 dpns can hold.

Rnd 1: K24, pm, K24.
Rnd 2: K all sts.
Rnd 3: K23, M1, K2, M1, K23. (50 sts)
Rnd 4: Work short rows.

Short Rows

The short rows are worked on both sides of the marker. Work all of them now and each time they are notated below.

K to 6 sts past marker, w&t, P12, w&t, K6 (you should be at marker now).

K10, w&t, P20, w&t, K10 (you should be at marker now).

K14, w&t, P28, w&t, K14 (you should be at marker now).

K18, w&t, P36, w&t, K to EOR.

Rnd 5: K all sts.
Rnd 6: K24, M1, K2, M1, K24. (52 sts)
Rnd 7: Work short rows.
Rnd 8: K all sts.
Rnd 9: K25, M1, K2, M1, K25. (54 sts)
Rnd 10: Work short rows.
Rnd 11: K all sts.
Rnd 12: K26, M1, K2, M1, K26. (56 sts)
Rnd 13: Work short rows.
Rnd 14: K all sts.
Rnd 15: K27, M1, K2, M1, K27. (58 sts)
Rnd 16: Work short rows.
Rnd 17: K all sts.
Rnd 18: K28, M1, K2, M1, K28. (60 sts)
Rnd 19: Work short rows.
Rnd 20: K all sts.
Rnd 21: K29, M1, K2, M1, K29. (62 sts)
Rnd 22: Work short rows.
Rnd 23: K all sts.
Rnd 24: K30, M1, K2, M1, K30. (64 sts)
Rnd 25: Work short rows.
Rnd 26: K all sts.

Rnd 27: K31, M1, K2, M1, K31. (66 sts)
Rnd 28: Work short rows.
Rnd 29: K all sts.
Rnd 30: K32, M1, K2, M1, K32. (68 sts)
Rnd 31: Work short rows.
Rnd 32: K all sts.
Rnd 33: K33, M1, K2, M1, K33. (70 sts)
Rnd 34: Work short rows.
Rnd 35: K all sts.
Rnd 36: K34, M1, K2, M1, K34. (72 sts)
Rnd 37: Work short rows.
Rnd 38: K all sts.
Rnd 39: K30, place next 12 sts on scrap yarn, join sts on both sides of scrap yarn together, K30. (60 sts)
Rnds 40–51: K all sts.

Place live sts on a piece of scrap yarn. Measure off about 10 armlengths of yarn, cut, roll into a ball, and place inside body.

Tail

Setup: Place 12 sts from scrap yarn at tail onto 2 dpns. Beginning at the bottom/center of the opening beneath the live sts, rejoin yarn and PU 4 sts along the left edge. K12 live sts. PU 4 more sts along the right edge. Tail should be stuffed a little at a time as you go (EOR). (20 sts)

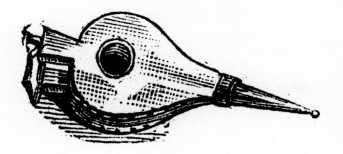

Rnds 1–5: K all sts.
Rnd 6: K2tog, K16, SSK. (18 sts)
Rnds 7–11: K all sts.
Rnd 12: K2tog, K14, SSK. (16 sts)
Rnds 13–17: K all sts.
Rnd 18: K2tog, K12, SSK. (14 sts)
Rnds 19–28: K all sts.
Rnd 29: K2tog, K10, SSK. (12 sts)
Rnds 30–64: K all sts.
Rnd 65: K2tog, K8, SSK. (10 sts)
Rnd 66: K all sts.
Rnd 67: K2tog, K6, SSK. (8 sts)
Rnd 68: K all sts.
Rnd 69: K2tog, K4, SSK. (6 sts)

Cut yarn, thread through remaining live sts, and pull closed. Weave in loose end.

Head

Setup: With RS facing, count 17 sts to the left of the first CO st. Beginning in the 18th st, PU a total of 48 sts with 3 dpns in the original CO sts (EOR).

Rnd 1: K all sts.
Row 2: K6, w&t, P12, w&t, K6.
Row 3: K8, w&t, P16, w&t, K8.
Row 4: K10, w&t, P20, w&t, K10.
Row 5: K12, w&t, P24, w&t, K12.
Row 6: K14, w&t, P28, w&t, K14.
Row 7: K16, w&t, P32, w&t, K16.
Row 8: K18, w&t, P36, w&t, K18.
Row 9: K16, w&t, P32, w&t, K16.
Row 10: K14, w&t, P28, w&t, K14.
Row 11: K12, w&t, P24, w&t, K12.
Row 12: K10, w&t, P20, w&t, K10.

Rnd 13: K4, SSK, K2tog, K12, SSK, K4, K2tog, K12, SSK, K2tog, K4. (42 sts)

Rnd 14: K all sts.

Rnd 15: K3, SSK, K2tog, K10, SSK, K4, K2tog, K10, SSK, K2tog, K3. (36 sts)

Rnd 16: K all sts.

Rnd 17: K2, SSK, K2tog, K24, SSK, K2tog, K2. (32 sts)

Rnd 18: K all sts.

Rnd 19: K1, SSK, K2tog, K22, SSK, K2tog, K1. (28 sts)

Rnd 20: K all st.

Rnd 21: SSK, K2tog, K18, w&t, P16, w&t, K18, SSK, K2tog. (24 sts)

Rnd 22: K all sts.

Rnd 23: (SSK) 6 times, (K2tog) 6 times. (12 sts)

Rnd 24: K all sts.

Rnd 25: (SSK) 3 times, (K2tog) 3 times. (6 sts)

Cut yarn, thread through remaining live sts, pull closed. Weave in loose end. Add safety nose (if using), inserting post through the center of the sts in Rnd 25.

Stuff head and tail only now.

Closing Body

Place 60 sts from scrap yarn onto 3 dpns; join in the round.

Rnd 1: (K2tog, K4) 10 times. (50 sts)
Rnd 2: K all sts.
Rnd 3: (K2tog, K3) 10 times. (40 sts)
Rnd 4: K all sts.
Rnd 5: (K2tog, K2) 10 times. (30 sts)
Rnd 6: K all sts.

Stuff remainder of body, using a dpn from the outside to help shift the stuffing where you want it. Stuff fully, rounding out the back.

Rnd 7: (K2tog, K1) 10 times. (20 sts)
Rnd 8: K all sts.
Rnd 9: (K2tog) 10 times. (10 sts)

Cut yarn, thread through remaining live sts, and pull closed. Weave in loose end.

Wrap tail alongside of body in front of your cat and even with the bottom of the body, stretching it slightly so that it ends up on the opposite side of head. Seam in place along the bottom edge and at the bottom of the head, pulling it up to the body.

Ears (make 2 the same)

The ears are worked separately and seamed to head. Work begins at bottom of ear. CO 15 sts onto 3 dpns; join in the round.

Rnds 1–2: K all sts.
Rnd 3: K1, SSK, K2tog, K5, SSK, K2tog, K1. (11 sts)
Rnds 4–5: K all sts.
Rnd 6: SSK, K2tog, K3, SSK, K2tog. (7 sts)
Rnds 7–8: K all sts.
Rnd 9: K2tog, K3, SSK. (5 sts)

Cut yarn, thread through remaining live sts, pull closed. Flatten ear with first CO st in the center/front; decreases on the sides. Create a slight hollowing in the front and seam to head with hollowing pointed forward/outward just behind the first decreases on each side.

Front Leg (make 1 only)

CO 18 sts onto 3 dpns; join in the round.

Rnds 1–5: K all sts.
Rnd 6: K2tog, K14, SSK. (16 sts)
Rnds 7–16: K all sts.
Row 17: K2, w&t, P4, w&t, K2.
Row 18: K3, w&t, P6, w&t, K3.

Row 19: K4, w&t, P8, w&t, K4.
Rnd 20: K2tog, K12, SSK. (14 sts)
Rnds 21–40: K all sts.
Row 41: K9, w&t, P4, w&t, K9.
Row 42: K9, w&t, P4, w&t, K9.
Rnd 43: K all sts.

Cut yarn, thread through remaining live sts, pull closed. Weave in loose end. Stuff paw and leg up to the first 5 rounds. Flatten the first 5 rounds and seam CO edge to body with paw covering face. If needed to hold leg in place, the top 1 in./2.5 cm on each side can also be seamed to body. Bend paw forward/downward.

Acknowledgments

I was lucky enough to have the support of three different yarn companies while working on this book. Thank you to Cascade Yarns, Berroco, and Woolfolk Yarn for the wonderful range of fibers, colors, and yarn weights I had at my fingertips!

Thank you to the kind people who let me photograph cats in their locations: Karen Kincaid Brady at the Neill-Cochran House Museum in Austin, Texas; Gina Walker at the Gruene Mansion Inn, Gruene, Texas; Eliseo Mantanez at the Commodore Perry Estate, Austin, Texas; the Harrie P. Woodson Memorial Library in Caldwell, Texas; Fast Eddie's Sports Tavern and Social Club, Austin, Texas; and the John and Betsy Sailors home in Cedar Park, Texas.

I have the greatest group on Ravelry. Thank you to the 40+ people who volunteered to test knit, as well as everyone in the group for your continued support of my designs and of me personally all these years.

And to my husband, Mark, the best photographer's gopher there could ever be. Thank you for all your trips up and down the stairs, carrying cats.

About the Author

Sara Elizabeth Kellner is the designer of Rabbit Hole Knits—toy and animal patterns for hand knitters—and author of *Wild and Woolly Knitted Animals*. Her goal when designing is to create patterns that portray the animals realistically while still evoking the personality of each, a twinkle in their eyes, and the question "Did I just see that animal move?" on the lips of every knitter.

Dona nobis pacem